Oral History

Oral History
A Guide for Teachers
(and Others)

THAD SITTON, GEORGE L. MEHAFFY, & O. L. DAVIS, JR.

University of Texas Press, Austin

Copyright © 1983 by the University of Texas Press
All rights reserved
Printed in the United States of America
First Edition, 1983

Requests for permission to reproduce material
from this work should be sent to Permissions,
University of Texas Press, Box 7819, Austin, Texas 78712.

Library of Congress Cataloging in Publication Data
Sitton, Thad, 1941–
    Oral history.
    Bibliography: p.
    1. Oral history—Handbooks, manuals, etc.   I. Mehaffy,
George L.   II. Davis, O. L. (Ozro Luke), 1928–
III. Title.
D16.14.S57   1983   907'.1273   83-3483
ISBN 0-292-76026-4
ISBN 0-292-76027-2 (pbk.)

Contents

Oral History

Daily our grandfathers are moving out of our lives taking with them, irreparably, the kind of information contained in this book. And it isn't just happening in Appalachia. . . .

The big problem, of course, is that since these grandparents were primarily an oral civilization, information being passed through the generations by word of mouth and demonstration, little of it is written down. When they're gone, the magnificent hunting tales, the ghost stories that kept a thousand children sleepless, the intricate tricks of self-sufficiency acquired through years of trial and error, the eloquent and haunting stories of suffering and sharing and building and healing and planting and harvesting—all these go with them, and what a loss.

If this information is to be saved at all, for whatever reason, it must be saved now; and the logical researchers are the grand-children. . . .

Eliot Wigginton, *The Foxfire Book*, 1972

1 / Introduction

Oral history is in the air, and even without benefit of manuals like
this one, classroom oral history projects are currently under way in
many American public schools. This is important to understand at
the onset, because it is one of the things that makes our how-to-do-it
manual different from most. We are not so much telling teachers
what they *should* do as we are drawing together, from many sources,
a systematic account of what they are already doing. Unlike many
educational innovations, the idea of classroom oral history began
with practicing teachers in real-world classrooms and, up to this
point, has spread largely by word of mouth and example. The oral
history project is a grass-roots teaching innovation by teachers and
for teachers, and our book has been written with this fact in mind.
Oral History: A Guide for Teachers (and Others) is the first full-length
handbook of oral history designed specifically for in-service and pre-
service teachers. Our purpose is to assimilate our personal experiences in oral history, as well as the collective experience of hundreds
of pioneering classroom teachers, into a practical guide to aid others.

As will become clear later on, the classroom oral history project
may take many forms, but all of these involve two key elements. In
the first place, and however modest they may be, oral history programs involve students in an active, rather than passive, approach to
the study of history. Students become their own historians for the
very best of reasons: they are engaged in live research and they are
exploring unknown ground. Second, student oral history projects are
pursued in part outside of the classroom setting. The universe in
which oral history operates is the face-to-face social world of the students' home community, the world students are familiar with. This
local emphasis can provide a useful corrective for the "big picture"
history of textbooks. The schoolroom oral history project can "bring
history home." [1]

That is to say, classroom oral history involves oral history fieldwork, and here, at the beginning, is a good place to take a first look at what this may mean. The following accounts from the student oral history projects *Tsa'Aszi* (Ramah, New Mexico) and *Foxfire* (Rabun Gap, Georgia) come from very different regional cultures, but they tell us important things about the nature of oral history fieldwork and the impact it may have upon students. The cultural context of *Tsa'Aszi* is Navaho, while the *Foxfire* project is based in the Appalachian South, but these descriptions may typify the research experiences of students and teachers at hundreds of other functioning oral history projects in the United States.

The teacher-adviser at the Ramah School describes one student's part of the *Tsa'Aszi* project:

> To gather our material we go to peoples' houses. For example, Paul wanted to write about old wagons, so he asked around to find out who might know the most. An elderly man named Antonio Martinez was thought to be a likely source. So we got our questions, tape recorders and cameras ready and with four other young men, set out to find him. A four-wheel drive vehicle is absolutely necessary to travel over the ruts. He lived several miles south of the school, which is centrally located on the Ramah reservation, but many, many miles from any town, and his hogan was located somewhere in this vast land, isolated from any other dwellings except the hogans of his daughters or grandchildren "just over the hill." Since it was winter, they were home when we arrived, and welcomed us because some were of the same clan.
>
> Their hogan was quite old. The logs were ash grey, the mud roof quite high from years of adding another layer. The mud had become like adobe after the many years in the sun. To go inside the hogan it was necessary to step down a foot and a half, the dirt floor lowered after generations of being walked on. . . . It was winter, snow on the ground, and still cold from the night inside, even though the wood burning stove was blazing and probably had been all night. Outside, the sun was bright and it was comfortable enough to be in shirt sleeves, even though the temperature was low. Mr. Martinez welcomed us, but was quite curious as to what we wanted and to what our equipment was. Alvin explained it to him and we sat on our haunches while Mr. Martinez told us everything he knew about wagons, at great length, while we listened quietly, asking questions only when he had finished speaking.
>
> We then went to take pictures. Many, many generations of his family had lived here before him, and there were old things that had been there for years, well preserved by the arid climate.

We took pictures of the old wagons, of old handmade saddles, bridles, farming tools, fences, kitchen utensils and so forth, being careful to leave them as is.

Over the hill, at a son's home, there were some other wagons, so we drove over there. Some of the students took pictures, while another talked to an old man, older than Mr. Martinez, who was in the horse corral pulling the stalks off of ears of summer corn. . . .

The pace of the morning was slow and the space around their house enclosed only by distant mesas, nearby hills and pinon pine. The only smells were sunshine, sweet pine, and strong coffee, peaceful aromas fitting with the sounds of birds and the soft throaty huskiness of the Navaho language.

We returned to the school to put the words into writing. . . . The interview is in Navaho, but the initial transcription is done in English, as rapidly as possible, because Navaho is a difficult language to write. But proofreading verifies the accuracy. It is then translated into Navaho and then written into an article in English. Students seem oblivious to being the first generation of Navahos who are easily fluent in both languages.[2]

Another brief account by a *Foxfire* staff member offers a student's-eye view of a similar enterprise (and, incidentally, suggests something of what *Tsa'Aszi*'s Navaho field researchers may have felt).

It wasn't until I had worked on *Foxfire* for five months that an inexplicable void between myself and the old people of our region disappeared. The void was mysterious, but it still existed. Maybe it was instilled hostilities toward older generations. Maybe it was the fact that I just couldn't see their importance or the relevance of what they had to say to the way I live today.

Then I met Aunt Arie. It was a cold day, and I can remember the jeep traveling far back into a remote area. I was apprehensive because I didn't know what to expect. Her log cabin was a time machine taking me into the eighteen-eighties. Everything she had—from the stern-looking pictures of her grandparents to the fireplace that was her only source of heat—made me stop and look deeply for the first time.[3]

But we are getting ahead of ourselves and leaving many questions unanswered. In our imagination we think we have heard at least some of the following points raised: What is oral history, anyway, and why is it a reputable way of doing historical research? How does it relate to classrooms, students, and the formal curriculum? Don't teachers have enough to cover already? What's more, how is oral history to be reconciled with the current emphasis on basic skills? Isn't it a little frivolous for this era of back to basics? What are some good, hard, justifiable reasons for involving classes in oral history projects? Perhaps we are guilty of putting words in teachers' mouths, but these seem to be reasonable questions that teachers would expect us to deal with in our introduction. Our book is designed to be practical rather than theoretical, concrete rather than abstract—a nuts and bolts handbook about planning and implementing classroom oral history projects. When it comes to justifying a new project to a departmental chairperson, principal, or school board, theory is sometimes very practical! Teachers are often relatively autonomous in regard to what goes on within the four walls of their classroom, but oral history, almost by definition, is a fieldwork enterprise that opens new relationships between the world of classroom and history textbook and the oral traditional history of the community outside. This is hardly business as usual. These questions, as well as the anticipated questions of authoritative others, need to be answered—now.

What is oral history? It is both one valid research procedure of the historian at work and, in a secondary sense, the forms of historiography created by that research. "History" is one of those everyday words with a confusion of meanings. In one meaning, history is everything that happened in the human past. In another sense it is the debris, the traces, left by that happening, which take the forms of written documents, artifacts, and the recollections of living persons. Working with the evidence embodied in document, artifact, and memory, the historian labors to craft history in the third and most familiar sense—the forms of historiography, which include biographies, political narratives, textbooks, and the like; history as it appears on the bookshelf.

Oral history is the recollections and reminiscences of living people about their past. As such, oral history is subject to all the vagaries and frailties of human recall; yet, in this respect, it is not substantially different from history as a whole, which is often distorted, subjective, and viewed through the screen of contemporary experience. The materials of oral history are the raw data of historical scholarship—history as primary sources with the warts, wrinkles, and inconsistencies still in place. Rich in personal triumph and tragedy, it is a history of the common person, the undocumented but not inarticulate. As a general scholarly phenomenon, oral history is expanding the limits of our historical knowledge, particularly in the area of social history, but as a narrative process, it is as old as history itself.[4]

In fact, oral history is nothing very new. The Greek historian Herodotus, the so-called father of history, worked mainly with the personal recollections of living participants in the events he described. In preliterate societies (and in the preliterate antecedents of our own society) history was oral tradition, held only in living memory and passed down from generation to generation in narrative, folktale, ballad, and epic verse.

In modern times, however, historians have strongly preferred to create their histories from documentary evidence alone and have tended to neglect the evidence contained in artifacts or in living oral tradition. By the late nineteenth century, history had largely become a "science of documentary analysis," as one practitioner described it, and scholarly historians looked with great distrust upon the historical evidence of oral tradition. Oral testimony about the past was regarded as unreliable and subjective, even as unworthy of being taken into account.

By the 1950s, two key technological developments, the telephone and the tape recorder, operating in very different ways, were helping to stimulate new interest in oral tradition as historical evidence. A number of historians (notably Allan Nevins at Columbia University) began to argue that modern communications media, especially the telephone, were drastically restricting the creation of such valuable personal documents as the letter and diary. Technological changes were creating a significant gap in the historical record, and this gap was widest in the critical area of personal communications—letters, memoirs, and the like.

Technology caused the problem but, according to Nevins, technology could help to fill the gap in the historical evidence. The oral history project Nevins began at Columbia University was designed to use the recently perfected audio tape recorder to interview significant men and women in American political and social life and to create from those interviews an "oral document." As Michael Frisch notes, "American oral history came into its own through Allan Nevins' project at Columbia, the main focus of which was on political and diplomatic history, and the main work of which was the debriefing of the Great Men before they passed on. Its nature was explicitly archival, informational, and elitist."[5]

But if modern oral history began with a conservative attempt to create a replacement "personal document" for the private letter and to focus upon the doings of important persons, it soon began to lead historians in different directions. One of these directions led to a reawakened interest in the history of the classes, ethnic enclaves, and occupation groups in American society that create few documentary records and that consequently had received little space in the formal histories. In the 1960s and 1970s there were oral historical studies of mill workers, coal miners, and black tenant communities in the South. And the "short and simple annals of the poor" often turned out to be anything but that when people were confronted with a tape recorder and invited to tell their side of the story.

In fact, the power of this telling was sometimes quite remarkable. The case of Nate Shaw, an illiterate black sharecropper, typifies many such examples. Early in 1969, historian Theodore Rosengarten and a friend were investigating a defunct organization called the Alabama Sharecroppers' Union, and they discovered that Shaw had been a principal actor in a legendary confrontation between union members and the local sheriff's deputies in 1932, which resulted in Shaw spending twelve years in an Alabama prison. Although he could neither read nor write, Shaw proved to be an extraordinary historical informant about the affairs of the Alabama Sharecroppers' Union and about all the experiences of his long life. He was a powerful storyteller with an excellent memory, who could recount in minute detail events that had taken place sixty years before. Rosengarten returned to Shaw again and again, and gradually the idea of editing his oral life history evolved. Scores of interview hours and thousands of transcript pages culminated in 1974, when Shaw's story was published as *All God's Dangers: The Life of Nate Shaw*, a work that subsequently won the National Book Award. H. J. Geiger of the *New York Times Book Review* describes this remarkable work:

> Nate Shaw strides directly off the page and into our consciousness, a living presence, talking, shouting, sorrowing, laughing, exulting, speaking poetry, speaking history. We come to know Nate Shaw the farmer, hunter, log cutter, lumber hauler, swamp drainer, house builder, mule trainer, bee keeper, hog raiser, blacksmith, maker of axe handles, basket weaver. Nate Shaw is a primary source . . . a black Homer, bursting with his black Odyssey.[6]

As one may judge from this reaction, the historical products of oral history can be powerful stuff, and it is not surprising that oral history seems to be gradually reshaping our views of the recent American past. Nate Shaw, for instance, hardly approximates conventional scholarly interpretations of the downtrodden tenant farmer. Likewise, careful historical reconsideration of the remarkable Federal

Writers' Project slave narratives, recorded in the 1930s, is changing our views about the institution of slavery. Some highly respected historians are even arguing that we should begin to rethink and rewrite American history upward from the organizational units of families and local communities, rather than downward from a strictly nationalistic perspective. This is the view of David J. Russo in *Families and Communities: A New View of American History*.

In addition to stimulating a new interest in families, communities, and the undocumented segments of American society, the rise of oral history has triggered a quest for new varieties of social history and for new and closer relationships between history and the other social sciences, notably folklore, cultural anthropology, and sociology.

For example, in *Everything in Its Path: Destruction of Community in the Buffalo Creek Flood*, Kai T. Erikson combined the methodologies and topical interests of sociology and oral history for a fascinating account of the great Buffalo Creek disaster in Kentucky in 1974 and of the way in which this event later haunted the lives of the survivors. On the other hand, William Lynwood Montell's *The Saga of Coe Ridge* fruitfully merged the research methods of oral history and folklore to reconstruct a factual account of ninety years in the life of the black mountain settlement of Coe Ridge, Kentucky. Settled in a remote Appalachian cove in the decade after the Civil War, Coe Ridge became a haven for former slaves, Indians, and a few outcast whites. It produced a coffee-skinned race of fiercely independent mountain folk, moonshiners, and outlaws, who became involved in recurrent feuds with their Anglo-Saxon neighbors. Montell collected the oral traditions of Coe Ridge's last inhabitants, who had moved away to urban centers in the 1940s and 1950s, and analyzed the large body of folkloric material—ballads, folktales, and the like—that was still available about the legendary settlement. He used these oral traditions and folklore to piece together a vivid story of the authentic rise and fall of the Coe Ridge community.

Several examples might be given of the current rapprochement of oral history with anthropology, but one of the most interesting is *Montaillou: The Promised Land of Error* by French medievalist Emmanuel Le Roy Ladurie. Published in 1979, *Montaillou* is a clear case of anthropological oral history from the fourteenth century! During the early 1300s, the remote village of Montaillou in the French Pyrenees became a hotbed for the heresy of Catharism. The local Catholic bishop conducted a lengthy inquisition of the heresy, during which peasants from the village and surrounding countryside were closely interrogated about their beliefs and behaviors. The peasants' replies were written down verbatim by papal clerks and the transcripts were stored for hundreds of years in Vatican archives. Ladurie used these oral history transcripts to write an anthropological history of the village of Montaillou, a detailed cultural reconstruction of nearly every aspect of daily life of the medieval French peasantry. Topics covered went far beyond the usual range of historical interests to include food habits and table manners, animal husbandry, sexual mores, even body language. *Montaillou* is a fascinating exploration in anthropological oral history, based upon transcripts that just happen to be six hundred years old!

In other studies, anthropological historians (usually termed "ethnohistorians") have documented the orally communicated history of many non-Western societies around the world and in the process have produced powerful evidence for the potential value of human memory as historical evidence. As Barbara Allen and Lynwood Montell note,

> the argument that the human memory cannot be trusted has been disproved by research among groups of people around the world who have a marked propensity for retaining historical truths over long periods of time. Ethnohistorians have demonstrated the veracity of orally communicated history among American Indians, Africans, and South Asian groups whose cultures are overwhelmingly oral and rich in ancient historical traditions. . . . The Icelandic family sagas, for instance, were transmitted orally for hundreds of years among a people who had lived for generations in one place, who had strong emotional identification with familiar landscapes, and who trained young people with a propensity for storytelling in the art of the saga.[7]

Finally, the rise of oral history has been associated with the publication of a variety of popular works based upon oral testimony, all part of a general surge of interest in humanly interesting, documentary accounts of real people's lives. The books of Studs Terkel have been in the forefront of this popular movement. In *Hard Times: An Oral History of the Great Depression*, Terkel put together an anthology of oral recollections about the Depression that communicated a vivid sense of what it meant to live through this great American crisis. In *Division Street: America*, Terkel's informants recount the evolution of their neighborhood in inner city Chicago, and in *Working: People Talk about What They Do All Day and How They Feel about*

What They Do, Terkel took a detailed oral history snapshot of American work attitudes during the mid twentieth century.

Another of the most influential works of popular oral history is Alex Haley's *Roots*, in which Haley successfully traced the history of his family through generations of slavery back to the family's African origins. At the beginning of Haley's decade-long quest were family oral traditions about an African named Kunta Kinte and some words in an unknown West African language. Haley's *Roots* was a big publishing success, as was the TV miniseries based on the book, and both book and TV drama gave additional impetus to popular oral history.

Finally, among the most successful recent works of popular oral history are *The Foxfire Book* and its successors, and at this point our discussion of the rise of oral history returns to teachers, students, and the central topic of this book—classroom oral history.

Foxfire had its origins in the English and journalism classes of a single teacher in rural North Georgia. Frustrated with the curricular status quo, Eliot Wigginton and his students at Rabun Gap-Nacoochee School in Rabun Gap, Georgia, began publishing a popular magazine of community oral history, folklore, and folklife. Wigginton served as project adviser, but the students themselves did the work. With cameras and tape recorders in hand, students field-collected the raw materials for their journal from the living repositories of the old mountain culture. Then they transcribed and edited their field data into articles with titles like "Moonshining as a Fine Art," "Log Cabin Construction," and "Planting by the Signs." Student motivation was high, community acceptance of the journal was excellent, and *Foxfire* was launched.[8]

With little financial support from its school, *Foxfire* struggled for existence during the years 1967 through 1972. This period of financial hard times ended abruptly in 1972, when a college friend of Wigginton persuaded Doubleday to publish the first anthology from *Foxfire* as *The Foxfire Book*. This work was dedicated "To the people of these mountains in the hope that, through it, some portion of their wisdom, ingenuity and individuality will remain after them to touch us all." *The Foxfire Book* was pungently subtitled "hog dressing; log cabin building; mountain crafts and foods; planting by the signs; snake lore; hunting tales; faith healing; moonshining; and other affairs of plain living."

If this was "plain living" the American public was ready for it. Doubleday's modest expectations were immediately confounded as

The Foxfire Book sold 100,000 copies in the first month after publication and shot to the top of the nonfiction book lists. Total sales for the first *Foxfire* anthology now approach four million copies, and the combined sales of subsequent *Foxfire* books total several million more. These anthologies include *Foxfire 2* (1973), *Foxfire 3* (1975), *Foxfire 4* (1977), *Foxfire 5* (1979), *Foxfire 6* (1980), and *Foxfire 7* (1981).

In addition, Doubleday has published successful oral history anthologies from two of *Foxfire*'s descendants—*The Salt Book* (from *Salt*, Kennebunkport, Maine, 1977, edited by Pamela Wood) and *Bittersweet Country* (from *Bittersweet*, Lebanon, Missouri, 1978, edited by Ellen Gray Massey)—and reportedly plans another, based upon the several *Foxfire*-concept magazines presently operating in Alaska. Finally, *I Wish I Could Give My Son a Wild Raccoon* (edited by Eliot Wigginton), an anthology of oral history interviews from over thirty *Foxfire*-concept journals across the country, was published in 1976. A very significant fraction of the revenues of one of America's largest publishers now derives from these student-produced oral history materials!

The *Foxfire* story is perhaps fairly well known. Much less familiar is the story of the general spread of *Foxfire*-concept oral history magazines since 1972. In 1977, a questionnaire study found eighty-four such publications; now the count stands at over two hundred. *Foxfire*-concept magazines (often called "cultural journalism") are scattered widely across the United States, functioning successfully within a wide range of community, school, and classroom circumstances, and at grade levels from middle school to junior college. There are inner-city publications like *Cityscape* and *Streetlight*, rural and small town projects like *Bittersweet*, *Loblolly*, and *Out of the Dark*, and suburban projects like *From Snake Hill to Spring Bank*. Because cultural journalism draws power from ethnic pride and sense of place, there is a wide range of culturally distinctive *Foxfires*. These include *Tsa'Aszi* (Navaho), *Kalikaq Yugnek* (Eskimo), *Sombras del Pasado* (Mexican American), *Nanih Waiya* (Choctaw), *Mo'Olelo* (Hawaiian), and *Lagniappe* (Cajun/Creole).

On the face of it, *Foxfire*-type journals seem to be an unlikely educational phenomenon in this era of back to basics, but part of the mystery is dispelled if we recognize that the journals are primarily functioning as "public history." Public history is another offshoot of the rise of oral history, and has been defined by some of its practitioners as "historical researches conducted in the community for public benefit, outside of academic environs."[9] At the *Foxfire*-concept magazines, student fieldworkers go into the home communities to collect oral history interviews, photographs, and documentary materials relative to their topics, and then process these historical data into forms of popular history designed for community use.

Crude as these first products may often be, community acceptance is often both immediate and impressive. As a final note on the schoolroom descendants of *Foxfire*, Gail Parks of the National Rural Center captures some of the dynamics of this community response.

> An exciting thing happens in small towns and rural areas when the first issue of a Foxfire-concept magazine appears in grocery stores and lunch counters. It sells out the first day. Most projects underestimate the public response and have to reprint. As a result, project students and advisors gain a buoyant sense of self esteem from community people, who seem to feel greater self esteem as a result of the magazine. It is almost a magic formula, given honest work.[10]

To reiterate, oral history is both as old as human speech and a new and innovative breakthrough in the process of researching and writing history. Oral history is a rapidly expanding methodology that is causing major readjustments in the way we look at the American past, and one which is moving academic history closer to the methods and topical concerns of other fieldwork social sciences. In *Hard Times*, *Working*, *Roots*, *All God's Dangers*, *Foxfire*, and numerous other recent works, writers have used the methodology of oral history to create new forms of popular history of immense interest to the general public.

But why all this concern with oral history? There have been few serious attempts to explain the oral history phenomenon in American society, but the most thoughtful to date is that of Tamara K. Hareven in the journal *Daedalus*. Hareven defined the process as a "search for generational memory."

> Why this exercise of "tribal rites" in an advanced technological society? Today, when the printing and circulation of information have reached an all-time peak, and when computers generate and objectify knowledge, scholars, foundations and cultural organizations, and the general public are reviving genealogy and the oral tradition—the tools of transmission of collective memory in nontechnological societies. Among scholars, this revival represents a revolt against "objective" social science and a shift from an emphasis on strictly formal knowledge to existential process. Oral history and the search for roots also fit into the

effort of recent scholarship to integrate the experience of large segments of the population into the historical and sociological record. On a more popular level, the oral history revival is connected with an effort to authenticate the experiences of different ethnic groups in American culture. It thus represents a commitment to pluralism and expresses the reemergence of ethnicity and its acceptance as a vital aspect of American culture.[11]

Not surprisingly, this search for generational memory by way of oral history has spawned a wide range of informal experimentation with oral history in the public schools. The two hundred or so *Foxfire*-concept journals seem but the tip of the iceberg in schoolroom use of oral history, though one that has played a large role in further dissemination of the idea. Practicing teachers have seized upon oral history as something different, something genuinely new and exciting, and a powerful antidote to students' frequent apathy toward textbook studies of history. Within the last few years, the classroom oral history project has received the blessings of professional organizations of education and the editors of scholarly journals, but all of this has come after the fact. Classroom oral history was invented by practicing teachers, and has survived and spread because it works. It is as simple as that.

Classroom oral history serves to bridge the gap between curriculum and community; it brings history home by linking the world of textbook and classroom with the face-to-face social world of the student's home community. Far too often, students may get the idea that history is only a textbook thing, something that always happened long ago, far away, and to somebody else, having almost nothing to do with them. Textbooks, by their very nature, present the nationalist, big picture versions of history. What is needed is some corrective addendum to the big picture history of the textbooks, something that suggests to students that history is something all around them and from which they personally derive. This is what novelist William Faulkner may have meant when he observed that "people talk about the 'dead past.' The past is not dead. It's not even *past*."

Classroom oral history effectively promotes this insight by involving students in live historical research in the social world they know best, their families, ethnicities, and home communities. Does it take an oral history project of the scale of *Foxfire* to accomplish this? Hardly. An assignment for a series of life history interviews with a grandfather or grandmother can serve just as well—likewise, a modest classroom study of the local impact of the Great Depression or of the social aftermath of Vietnam. Possibilities abound, but how many of us have taught our textbook units on World War I and World War II while the men who went over the top at Belleau Wood, or hit the beach at Tarawa, were pumping gas a few blocks away? The observations of Eliot Wigginton haunt many of us, not excluding the authors of this book.

> The American history teacher who drags students through text explanations of the Depression, WPA camps, labor unions, or the World Wars, and ignores the fact that the community surrounding the school is full of people *who were there* is being almost criminally negligent. All the songs, the folklore, the experiences and the tales are left out, and what a loss.[12]

What a loss, indeed, but the simplest classroom oral history project can effectively tap these rich community resources for the study of history and, in the process, can particularize history and give it human meaning. Historical understanding is in part cognitive, intellectual, a mastery of dates, names, relationships, and causal sequences. But there is also an affective dimension to our understanding of the past, and it is in this area that oral history can make its greatest contribution. When we study history we vicariously experience what life was like in the past, as well as intellectually grasp the ordering of past events and the reasons why they occurred in the way they did. Textbooks do a good job with the sequencing and facts of history, but poorly convey the experiential "feel" of past events. Oral history projects in the local community can fill this affective gap in our teaching of history.

Granted, the past is past, and students and teachers (short of the time machine) will never actually experience the great Texas City harbor disaster of 1947, when a shipload of ammonium nitrate exploded and hundreds of people died. But which of these vicarious experiences of that event may offer the greatest real sense of what it was like to be present at that place and time: the textbook account of the explosion and fire, a collection of contemporary newspaper stories about the disaster, or a face-to-face classroom interview with a survivor? The answer seems obvious.

In *Death in Life*, an oral history of the survivors of the atomic bombing of Hiroshima, Robert Lifton has compiled a moving record of a far greater human disaster than the Texas City explosion. Estimates of how many died in Hiroshima range from sixty-five thousand to four hundred thousand, but, as James Hoopes observes, "such figures do not convey either the horror or meaning found in the spoken memories of a single survivor." [13]

> The appearance of people was . . . well, they had skin blackened by burns. . . . They had no hair because their hair was burned, and at a glance you couldn't tell whether you were looking at them from in front or in back. . . . They held their arms bent (forward) like this (he proceeded to demonstrate their position) . . . and their skin—not only on their hands, but on their faces and bodies too—hung down. If there had been only one or two such people . . . perhaps I would not have had such a strong impression. But wherever I walked I met these people. . . . Many of them died along the road—I can still picture them in my mind—like walking ghosts. They didn't look like people of this world. [14]

The projected statistics of nuclear war all pale beside this one fragment from oral tradition. One reason classroom oral history projects work is because they reconnect textbook with community, and the printed word with the experiences of living persons. In John Dewey's terms, oral history is a powerful strategy for reuniting "education and experience."

Classroom oral history projects can be more than just local history, even having application outside the formal boundaries of the discipline of history. Part of the reason for our frequent neglect of community resources for the study of history may be the assumption (built into our classifications of the curriculum) that community history can only be locally relevant, appropriate only for the state history course, if even for that. However, little thought is required to realize how patently false this notion is. World, national, and state history are convenient categories with which to classify social studies courses and textbooks, but they are hardly watertight compartments in the real world. The study of the local community and the study of the larger world beyond it are not mutually exclusive endeavors, any more than local history, United States history, and world history are really three different fields. Is there any doubt that students might study the Great Depression or World War II in Rabun Gap, Georgia, Gary, Texas, or anywhere else, by field interviews with persons who lived through those historical events? The local community is, after all, that part of the human social world that is available to public school students for direct, personal, and in-depth study. And, as previously suggested, that community holds a potential for experience that far transcends any classroom-based curriculum.

In any case, classroom teachers are currently experimenting with oral history fieldwork in a wide variety of curriculum areas: history, government, sociology, even areas quite outside the realm of social studies. Social studies teachers should recognize that good work in oral history is being done in English classrooms! That a project in oral history is applicable to subject areas other than social studies is attested to by the fact that it is being so applied. Such a project emerges as an effective strategy to make any subject area "community specific." [15]

Take English, for example. The oral life history, in which a student interviews a living subject and transcribes and edits those interviews into a coherent narrative, is as appropriate for English as it is for history. English classes, too, can collect a variety of oral literature from the living body of community lore in the forms of legends, "belief tales," ballads, jokes, riddles, and other folkloric genres. Integrated with formal coursework in literature, this material can open new possibilities for studying the folk origins of verbal art. Reading classes may tape-record the colorful oral autobiographies of community residents, and then transcribe, edit, and photocopy these interviews to create community-specific reading materials. This material then can be used to bridge the gap between the written and spoken word, and to effectively link the act of reading to the living language(s) of the community, whatever its cultural diversity.

Oral history has potential application to other disciplines as well, for example, home economics. In home economics, classroom-based projects may locate master practitioners of community folk arts and crafts, traditional skills with immediate relevance to the field. Such crafts include weaving, basketry, quilting, and food preservation, to name just a few. Craftspersons may be recorded on tape or film to incorporate their knowledge into the formal home economics curriculum, supplemented with other community-specific materials, to help preserve community folk crafts from oblivion.

It should be obvious that a similar argument may be made for the usefulness of oral history projects in industrial arts classrooms, or even for the teaching of agriculture. (Perhaps small-scale, intensive cultivation using animal power is not so obsolete as we once thought?) In any case, although this handbook is primarily intended for social studies teachers, there is clear indication that the potential applications of oral history go considerably beyond that field. Fieldwork projects are a powerful strategy for reuniting coursework and community in a variety of disciplines and, once again, the best support for this contention is that teachers are already doing it. This suppleness of application is another reason for the current popularity of classroom oral history.

Classroom oral history taps a personal motivation for the study of history by involving students in valid research within their own family, ethnic, and community heritage. In so doing, the oral history project builds students' sense of identification with this heritage and their feelings of self-worth. A professional historian named Carl Becker once argued that "everyman was his own historian."[16] Becker meant that the most basic use of historical studies may be to help individuals make sense out of their own lives by relating their life experience to the history of the home community and the larger world beyond it. According to Becker, historical interest naturally begins with the question, Who am I?, a question in part answered by another one, Where do I come from? (Who are my people, my community?). In this quest for personal identity every person is, by necessity, his or her own best historian.

For most persons (argued Becker), the natural progression of historical interest moves *outward* from this personal life experience, not *inward* from the remote and grandiose frameworks of national and international events, though this latter approach is, of course, the common strategy in the secondary schools. Indeed, according to Becker, we commonly teach our history backward, largely failing to tap the relevance of the discipline for our students' quest for self-identity. Viewed in this light, the classroom oral history project appears to offer a modest but useful corrective to this general tendency—a chance for students to serve as their own historians in exploring their most immediate and personal past.

What is more, with historical exploration of family and ethnic heritage often comes a heightened sense of self-worth. Part of the reason for the informal rise and spread of classroom oral history may be that such projects effectively bring students to know—and to celebrate—their own particular ethnic heritages. If the purpose of an ethnic studies curriculum is to right historical wrongs and to re-emphasize the importance of ethnic contributions in the American past, consider how important it must be to incorporate students' own immediate ethnic heritage in the instruction. Like textbook history in general, big picture ethnic studies run the risk of ending up too abstract and impersonal, too far from home. It would be far better for the black students to interview their own tenant grandfathers about the ingenious survival strategies of the tenant's yearly round (remember Nate Shaw?) than only to read some abstract account of tenantry in the textbook. For the purpose of increasing self-esteem, one can argue that the most effective ethnic studies curriculum is *always* community specific and personalized.

One community ethnic history project explored the process whereby this kind of localized ethnic studies curriculum might be created from scratch by the use of oral history. As a result of the project, many stories like that of Reverend S. L. Davis about his slave grandfather were recorded and set beside local Anglo oral traditions of black docility under slavery and the tenant system in a southern county.

> Don't think now, that this stubbornness just started yesterday. The black man, some of them, have been stubborn all his days. There's not a stripe was ever struck my grandfather. He told his boss, Ed Burleson, he says, "Listen, I'm going to work for you. That whip you got is for your animals, and the day you put that whip on me, that'll be the last man you put your whip on." He said, "I'm going to work, just tell me what you want done, and I'll do it. I know I belong to you, but you ain't going to put that whip on me." So Ed Burleson heard what he said, and Ed Burleson *believed* what he said.[17]

For the purposes of shifting attitudes and promoting black pride, we found this sort of ethnic studies material generally more effective than the obligatory passage in the American history text about Booker T. Washington and his uses of the sweet potato. The story proved even more compelling to that large segment of the local black school population that was personally acquainted with or related to Reverend Davis. Oral history projects work because they utilize a personal motivation for studying history and provide a powerful strategy for exploring—and celebrating—cultural diversity at its most grassroots level.

Classroom oral history projects develop both academic and interpersonal life skills of great usefulness to students, and in no way conflict with the current emphasis on back to basics. In his travels around the country, Eliot Wigginton had often defended oral history projects in general (and the *Foxfire* magazine in particular) against the charge that such projects run counter to an emphasis on basic skills. It is worthwhile to note what this battle-scarred veteran has to say on the matter.

> Is the subject, English, ignored in the process? Hardly. In fact, the opposite is true. English, in its simplest definition, is communication—reaching out and touching people with words,

sounds, and visual images. We are in the business of improving students' prowess in these areas. In their work with photography (which must tell the story with as much impact and clarity as the words), text (which must be grammatically correct except in the use of pure dialect from tapes they must transcribe), lay-out, make up, correspondence, art and cover design, selection of manuscripts from outside poets and writers—to say nothing of related skills such as fund raising, typing, retailing, advertising, and speaking at conferences and public meetings—they learn more about English than from any other curriculum I could devise. Moreover, this curriculum has built-in motivations and immediate and tangible rewards.[18]

Most classroom projects probably will not produce an oral history magazine like *Foxfire*, but many of the academic skills Wigginton enumerates are honed by the simplest of oral history exercises. For example, consider the case of the oral life history in which a student interviews an informant and edits the transcripts of this interview, or interviews, into an oral autobiography. The student must transcribe the material and struggle with the problem of ordering the oral testimony by punctuation and paragraph. A better inquiry lesson into the practical usefulness of such formal structures can scarcely be devised! The student edits the transcript for recurrent topics, and then cuts and splices the transcribed material to consolidate those topics. In the role of editor, the student struggles with basic structural decisions about what to omit and what to retain, and in what order to retain it. As in the interview process, the process of transcription and editing works as a form of experiential education, built around a series of naturally occurring problems that must be solved. During this part of the process, the skills being developed are not interactional and interpersonal but grammatical and literary—academic in the best sense of that term.

But what about the interactional and interpersonal skills developed by the oral history project? These seem life skills of equal value to the more conventionally academic ones, though skills rarely emphasized in social studies classrooms.

Oral history research is a kind of fieldwork, and field research methods are a systematic way to make social "sense" out of unfamiliar social settings in which the researchers are themselves participants. This is precisely the situation of any newcomer in a social setting, and the interactional process of oral history becomes an important life-skills training for students who must learn to make social sense out of a variety of unfamiliar social settings passed through in the course of their lives.

To reiterate, the "way of knowing," the structure of the discipline of fieldwork social science (oral history included) begins with personal participation in the setting under study, and the specific research techniques of fieldwork have been developed within the parameters of that personal involvement. Hence, unlike experimental research strategies, which may have relevance only to the laboratory, oral history fieldwork has direct application to the students' day-to-day life in society, their perennial career as social newcomers.

To help clarify what this means, we return to the oral life history example, this time to the interview phase that preceded transcription and editing, and consider the interpersonal skills being developed.

Interviewing is a complicated interactional process that improves greatly with practice. According to Lewis Dexter, a good interviewer has "as many of the virtues as possible of a good social scientist, a good reporter and a good historian."[19] Or, as Amelia Fry writes, the interviewer "should be that combination of journalist-historian, the Grand Inquisitor, Mata Hari, Sherlock Holmes, and one may add, Vanderbilt and Mellon."[20]

This is a large order, and probably never approached in the real world. But perhaps most social studies teachers would agree that modern American society is complicated enough, and deceptive enough, that a little "Sherlock Holmes" training is not a bad idea. This is not the place to analyze all the interactional elements that go into the life history interview, but the basic sequence may be sketched as follows: (1) locate the informant, persuade him or her to be interviewed, and set up the time and place; (2) conduct the background research to prepare appropriate questions for the first interview (topics to cover, sequencing, etc.); (3) during the first interview, interact with the informant in such a way as to maximize the relevant data he or she has to give; and (4) analyze the data collected to prepare for subsequent interviews.[21]

Interviewing is a complicated business, which is another way of saying that much is to be learned from it. During the interview process, students usually push their interactional skills well beyond their accustomed limits. They try to be the perfect, unobtrusive listener, while at the same time subtly directing the course of the interview. Keeping always in mind how the topic of the moment fits into the larger pattern of life history, interviewers probe for additional information. They try to say the least and get the most information in return, to ask the "perfect question" that will release the wellsprings of memory. The student interviewer is not the imperial director of the interview performance, or the ringmaster whipping the interviewees through their paces, but, rather, the *facilitator* of the process of memory. As this implies, the oral life history is an interactive product of both informant and interviewer.

Finally, there is a fourth stage in which novice interviewers listen to the tapes from the first interview, note all the things that they did wrong (or left out, or forgot to ask) and plot their strategy for subsequent life history interviews, but this should be enough discussion to make the point. The oral history project works because it teaches both academic and interpersonal life skills in a real-world, experiential context. Furthermore, modest though it may be, the classroom oral history project almost always is trying to *do* something. It is "for real" rather than "for drill," and the reality of project goals acts to transform the process of reaching them.

The classroom oral history project results in something of real value to families, community, school, and the larger world of historical scholarship. In fact, perhaps the most telling argument for the value of classroom oral history is that such projects are, in effect, real; they actually *do* something. They produce tangible products of personal and social value, and this, perhaps more than anything else, explains their unique potential to stimulate student enthusiasm and excitement.

The new social studies has emphasized mastery of process as a primary goal, the involvement of students in the ways of knowing that lie at the hearts of such disciplines as geography, economics, and history. Yet the process has often been essentially lifeless, as devoid of meaning as dropping a steel ball to test for gravity. The outcome is predictable, unremarkable, and known. What is lacking is reality. Students too often are perfectly aware that they are merely playacting scholarship in a play world, where nothing they do has any real effect and where it is unlikely they will discover anything that has not already been discovered.

But oral history is different. The promise of oral history is that it can involve students in real processes of discovery in search of valuable goals, and so combine process and product in a real experience. Students in oral history programs learn the craft of field research, gather interviews, edit and transcribe their tapes, and in the process produce a historical record. Students are not merely going through academic exercises, but are engaged in real processes of discovery that may result in historical works of real value to family and community.

This is our final point about the value of classroom oral history, and it concludes on a personal note. Some fifteen years ago a younger brother of one of the authors conducted a two-hour taped interview with his maternal grandfather. This was a classroom project in seventh grade state history required by a teacher who was obviously years ahead of her time! The grandfather told of growing up in absolute poverty in backwoods east Texas in the 1880s and 1890s, of attending pharmacy school on Galveston Island (narrowly escaping the great Galveston hurricane of 1900), of starting his own pharmacy in a small east Texas town, and of being wiped out by the Depression. His life story was interspersed with folklore—jokes, country aphorisms, mildly obscene anecdotes about Sam Houston, and a folk ballad about the tragic death of Jesse James (which he sang), entitled "The Dirty Little Coward that Shot Mr. Howard."

None of the rest of the family paid much attention to the interview at the time it was conducted, but in recent years, after the grandfather's death, they turned the ancestral homeplace upside down looking for the tape. The family would give a great deal for it. The brother and his grandfather had created a unique primary source from a part of the family history that was present only in the living memory of the grandfather. Now the tape and the memory that created it are both gone, and gone absolutely. As C. L. Sonnichsen has written, "The grassroots historian has a limited time to work before the night cometh, in which no man can work." [22]

Of the three general classes of historical evidence (documents, artifacts, and memories), evidence in the human memory is the most fragile and ephemeral. The oral history interview transforms fragile memory into a permanent record of the past that is both valuable and—given the passage of time—quite irreplaceable. And this is true of even the simplest classroom oral history project. Sooner or later to every oral historian, whether student or professional, comes the thought: "If I hadn't recorded this, it might have been lost forever."

So, oral history by its very nature yields tangible products of personal and social value. In recognition of this, one complete chapter of our handbook is given over to a discussion of the potential applications of classroom oral history and the ways in which the research data may be put to actual use. This deeply held belief, and the products chapter which is its concrete expression, is another way in which our book is different.

At this point, it is enough only to mention a few such possibilities. The classroom oral history project can result in family oral history tapes and transcripts, or in more elaborate oral life histories of family members. The project can produce community-specific curriculum materials to help reconnect textbook and community in several disciplines, and to serve as a permanent teaching resource in community schools. It can result in a community oral history archive, based in community or school libraries, or in a *Foxfire*-concept oral history magazine, published by the school for community use. Both these latter projects are really enterprises in the developing field of public history, "historic researches conducted in the community for public benefit, outside of academic environs."[23]

As we will see, there are other possibilities as well. The community oral history archive and the *Foxfire* magazine are ambitious, but far from unreasonable, outcomes of the classroom oral history project. The fact is, in ordinary classrooms from Clio, Alabama, to Chicago, Illinois, hundreds of such projects are already taking place.[24]

But enough said! At this point it seems reasonable to summarize "how we plan to get from here to there," as the old saying goes.

In chapter 2 we review the literature of classroom oral history, take a close look at the wide range of projects that have been attempted and offer several detailed case studies of functioning projects. Then, based upon the experience and example of existing projects, as well as our own ideas, we offer a typology of project options for the classroom teacher.

Our third chapter focuses on hardware, and in it we get down to brass tacks about the technical, as opposed to the interpersonal, side of oral history fieldwork. Topics include tape recorders, microphones, and recording procedures; interview outlines and preliminary research; field photography and the taking of field notes; storage, accession, and transcription of materials; and legal forms and procedures appropriate for the classroom project. We also present an up-to-date review of the rapidly developing technical side of oral history.

In chapter 4 we discuss the specifics of preparing students to become effective field researchers in oral history. To help accomplish this, we offer detailed training suggestions for the techniques of interpersonal relationships during the oral history interview. Central to the chapter is a discussion of the techniques and tactics of structured and unstructured interviewing, because these are the fieldwork strategies most appropriate to the classroom oral history project. But we go beyond the interview to briefly discuss other relevant fieldwork approaches, such as unobtrusive observation and participant observation. We argue that different approaches to oral history research, and different combinations of approaches, work best in different projects. Hence, we offer a comprehensive discussion of the whole dimension of interpersonal relations in fieldwork.

Basing our assertions upon the actual accomplishments of classroom oral history projects like *Foxfire* and others, we argue in chapter 5 that such projects may produce products of real educational and social value to families, schools, and communities and, furthermore, that the process skills of field research are probably best learned in pursuit of these socially real products. Potential products of classroom oral history are curriculum materials in local history, local studies, or ethnic studies; projects in public history such as oral history archives, oral history publications resembling *Foxfire* and other media productions for the community; and research studies of the historical dimensions of current problems in community political and social life. Again, modeled upon the actual accomplishments of functioning projects, this chapter considers some potential applications of classroom oral history in school and community.

Finally, in the appendixes we present a variety of reference tools of potential usefulness to the classroom project, including goals and guidelines for interviewers and interviewees, criteria for evaluating oral history interviews, and an extended discussion about *Foxfire*-concept magazine production.

2 / Project Options

Introduction to the Case Studies

What kinds of classroom projects are possible in oral history? We have suggested some of these in passing in the first chapter; now we would like to present a detailed discussion of project options. In the sections that follow, we offer a series of ten case studies of successful projects in classroom oral history and more than forty project ideas you might wish to consider. To suggest the true dimensions of the spectrum of classroom oral history—the range of project options—we have searched the literature, plumbed the ERIC microfiche system, picked the brains of every practicing teacher we know, and made full use of our own imaginations. But do these exhaust the possibilities? We very much doubt it, because we are continually hearing from practicing teachers of new ideas, new applications, of the supple methodology of oral history. Teachers should use this chapter to come up with their own ideas.

Because classroom oral history is in large measure a teacher invention and because teachers are very busy people, many oral history projects have never reached the literature. (For once in the field of education, performance has preceded rhetoric!) Because a lot of classroom oral history is "in fact" rather than "in print," we have talked to teachers and used our own imaginations about project possibilities. You should feel free to reject any given idea as too imaginative, and to take others with whatever grains of salt you think appropriate, but we warn you to be cautious about this. Our experience suggests that most, if not all, of the project options explored in this chapter are probably in actual practice somewhere in American classrooms.

In the section that immediately follows, the reality of the enterprise is not open to question. Here are nine detailed case descriptions of successful oral history projects, examples that illustrate the wide range of possibilities in classroom oral history.

"Oral History: The Family Is the Curriculum"
In Ruth Hirsch and Miriam Lewiger's sixth-grade classroom in New
Rochelle, New York, the family *became* the curriculum.' Students tape-
recorded interviews with parents, grandparents, great-grandparents,
great-aunts, and great-uncles and put together books about their
lives. Then they held an open house to honor those relatives and to
share the works that their lives had inspired. Brothers and sisters
were also invited to the open house, and about three hundred people between the ages of five and eighty-seven actually attended.

Students later wrote accounts about what they felt on the occa-
sion. One student wrote, "When my grandfather saw the book that I
wrote about him, he was filled with joy. He was so happy to see that
people cared." Another said that "it gave me great satisfaction to
know I could handle such a project. It really made me feel professional, carrying around a tape recorder and a folder marked 'oral
history.'" One girl wrote, "I found the real people. They said what was
inside. I learned so much I didn't know. I also found out that I'm not
the only one with inner thoughts. This interview—I'd rather call it a
trip to the inner person—has made me wiser. But most important it
has made me love these people more than ever."

According to the teachers, the project "concerned language arts
and social studies." Students were asked to write a book, based on
interviews with one of the oldest living members of their family. It
was begun before Thanksgiving to help students begin the interviewing at a time when families traditionally gather for the holidays and
reminisce about the family past. To arrive at appropriate questions to
ask, students listened to excerpts from *The Foxfire Book*, *Foxfire 2*,
and other works featuring oral life history accounts. These works
suggested questions that students adapted and modified for their interviews. Students were especially curious about such things as
houses, toys, and school. Questions were listed on the board as students thought of them, and the final list was reorganized and duplicated for the students to use during their interviews.

Many children used tape recorders, but others simply wrote out
the answers to their questions. Some collected information by letter
from relatives who lived abroad, and a few did telephone interviews.
On a holiday visit to Argentina, one girl taped an interview with her
grandmother in Spanish and then translated it into English for the
classroom project.

After completing the interviewing, many of the children chose to
transcribe their tapes word for word. Others summarized the answers. All the children were challenged by the necessity of reorganiz-

ing the materials to make a book other people would enjoy reading. Some used a question-and-answer form of organization; others organized the book chronologically or by important experiences in the lives of their subjects.

After the first drafts were written and proofread, students began to carefully type or hand copy the final versions. Notes about the author were detailed at this point for ultimate inclusion in the book, one girl noting that she was "11 and 10/12 years old and still unmarried." Many children added moving dedications. For example, one boy who interviewed his father, a victim of Nazi concentration camps, dedicated his book "to the memory of all the children who didn't survive the holocaust."

During the last stages of rewriting and reorganizing, students searched family attics and basements for old family photographs to include in the book. They rediscovered such long-neglected treasures as a grandfather's confirmation picture, a grandmother's graduation photo, and a great-grandparents' wedding portrait. After photos were selected, and in some cases original drawings made, the students learned how to bind their manuscripts as books.

On the date of the open house, parents, grandparents, and other relatives came to the school to examine the book about them for the first time. To help others share the material, students had posted excerpts from their books for them to read. One boy, whose book was about his mother, wrote of their birthplace in the Barbados: "We have beautiful beaches with white sand that glitters like silver in the moon and sun." Another quoted his French mother, "In Nice we had a French garden with pebbles and flower beds. One of the palm trees which is still there today is very tall, about 150 feet high. My father planted it when he was a boy." In one account, a relative told, "My salvation was coming to this country from Austria in 1905. This country was wonderful to us. I kissed the floor because I came here. That's how wonderful it is."

Families were deeply touched by the students' offerings and proud of their accomplishments. A grandfather, reading the biography of his mother and father, expressed the sentiments of many when he wrote to his grandson, "I was never so proud of a particular accomplishment as I was of yours."

"Americans in Vietnam"

In 1974, Beatrice Spade, an instructor in history at Louisiana State University, began an oral history project to record the experiences of Americans in Vietnam.[2] She was looking for some way to involve her students in live historical research in United States–Asian relations. The LSU library had scanty holdings in recent Asian history, and the community of Baton Rouge, Louisiana, had few persons of Asian heritage in residence, but the community—and the university itself—contained many Americans recently returned from the Vietnamese conflict. An oral history of their experiences seemed a logical idea.

From the beginning, this was much more than just an exercise. As Spade wrote, "Many servicemen participated in key historical events and could provide first hand accounts of their experiences. While few of them would take the time to write down their recollections, many of them probably would talk about what they had seen, heard, and felt in Asia."

In the spring of 1974, undergraduate students in Spade's classes volunteered to participate in the project to record the experiences of Americans in Vietnam. These students agreed to complete oral history interviews with at least three military veterans or personnel still on active duty, who had served in Vietnam at any time from the 1950s to the present. The student volunteers met together for an hour each week to learn oral history techniques, to plan strategies for contacting veterans, and to discuss information gained through interviews and reading.

The first half of the semester was given over to these training procedures. Students read Willa K. Baum's *Oral History for the Local Historical Society*, familiarized themselves with the cassette recorders and tapes to be used in the project, and conducted (or observed) a training interview with a "practice" veteran from the campus ROTC program.

As the training phase drew to a close, students began to contact Vietnam veterans who would act as informants. They approached friends that they knew had been in Vietnam, and used various strategies to locate veterans from farther afield. A display in the student union alerted other on-campus veterans to the project, and the campus newspaper, local newspapers, and a community television station carried stories describing it. In the end, preliminary contacts were made with several hundred potential informants.

But how to pick and choose among these? To help in the selection process, each veteran contacted was asked to fill out a questionnaire on his personal background, military training, and experience in Vietnam. In making their selections, students tried to choose a cross section of informants. "Clerks on the back lines who never even saw a mortar shell, marines with extensive combat experience, civil affairs personnel, pilots, ranking officers, grunts, all have their own

perspectives on the situation in Vietnam and can add a great deal to
the total picture." Students even kept charts, maps, and graphs showing how many informants had been interviewed from each branch of
the services, each rank, each specialty, each year, and each of the
various localities in Vietnam.

A period of background reading about the Vietnamese conflict
preceded the first interview, but many students quickly went back to
their books after it was over. They found that they simply needed
more information. As Spade notes, "This shortcoming was overcome
to some extent by the informants, who seemed to know what they
wanted to talk about and what they felt was important."

Interviews were scheduled in the veterans' houses or in suitable
rooms on campus, and each informant was interviewed in two approximately one-hour sessions. The amount of Vietnamese experience informants had to relate varied widely but, as a general practice,
splitting the interviewing into two sessions proved extremely useful.
The student interviewers had a chance to debrief their tapes with the
help of Spade or another student, to do background checks on points
raised in the first interview, and to determine what questions to ask
next. This interview-debrief-reinterview process proved highly effective in improving students' interviewing techniques and the quality of
their tapes. For one thing, they learned to ask fewer questions and
not to interrupt the flow of narrative.

Interviews were flexible, but students did follow a general format
of questioning. First, questions were asked about the informant's
background. Where was he born? What did his parents do? What was
his childhood like? When and why did he enter the service?

Then questions were asked about the informant's service training. What kind of training was it? How appropriate was it for what he
would experience in Vietnam? Did he have any advance training?

The third area of questioning related to the informant's actual
military experiences in Vietnam, and now the questions grew more
detailed. What happened to him when he first arrived in Vietnam?
Where was he assigned for duty? How long did it take him to reach
his assigned duty post? What was his function in the service? Would
he describe a normal day in his life in Vietnam? Would he relate any
experiences that stand out in his mind about the period of time he
was in Vietnam? Did he ever take part in any "special" (classified)
operations, and would he describe them? Could he describe in detail
any special device or weapon that he was handling, or that he encountered when in contact with the enemy?

Similar questioning sequences probed the additional areas of experiences with the indigenous peoples of Vietnam (the Army of the Republic of Vietnam [ARVN], civilian Vietnamese, the Montagnard peoples, etc.); experiences with prostitutes, drugs, and the black market; and attitudes toward officers, lower ranks (and other service groups), the Vietnamese, and the war in general.

Hard questions, but "in most instances the informants seemed to answer all the questions as honestly as they could." In many cases, and particularly so for those who had been in intense battle situations, informants were recalling very emotional experiences. Students had to be aware of the potential emotional impact of their questioning.

Enthusiasm generated by the project among students was quite high. In fact, two students continued to conduct interviews on their own time during the summer vacation after the semester project was ended. Students were even conducting interviews during the period of finals at the end of the semester—surely a rare occurrence! Completed interview tapes, questionnaires, and release forms were turned in to the university for permanent deposit with the Department of Archives, Louisiana State University. Students, teacher, and archivist all came to regard this material as valuable documentation of the U.S. experience in Vietnam. As Spade noted, "The interviews contain material which is valuable not only to historians, but also to those in other fields such as sociology, psychology, and military science."

From Beatrice Spade's perspective, there were other benefits, among them a permanent alteration in students' attitudes toward the study of history. Before the Vietnam War project, "Like stones skipping over the top of water, the ideas I projected in class rarely sank into the pool of a student's consciousness." Student attitudes changed greatly after interviews with those who actually lived through the Vietnam experience.

Spade came to believe that "Americans in Vietnam" was a project that could be replicated elsewhere, by almost any well-prepared college or high school class. She felt that it could be "implemented on a shoe-string budget, a huge budget, or no budget at all," and could be adapted for courses "in Southeast Asia history, American history, political science, and even sociology."

The Skewarkians

The Skewarkians is a classroom oral history project that never does the same thing twice—and with huge success.[3] Located in Martin County, North Carolina, the Skewarkians Junior Historians chapter is

sponsored by Elizabeth Roberson of the Bear Grass School in Wil-
liamstown. Bear Grass is a rural school of under three hundred students in grades 7–12. The entire eighth grade participates in the
Skewarkians project through Roberson's language studies/social studies block. Although the content of the project is included in the class,
much of the actual work takes place outside the school, during weekends or after school hours.

Since their beginning in 1978, the Skewarkians have accom-
plished a remarkable amount of research. One of their first projects
was an oral history book entitled *Smoke to Gold: The Story of Tobacco in Martin County*. This eighty-six-page, softbound publication
in local economic history has won no fewer than five state awards
and a national award from the American Association for State and
Local History, and has gone through several printings.

Research for *Smoke to Gold* was thorough by any standard. To
begin with, students were asked to go home and interview grandparents, aunts, and uncles about how tobacco used to be cultivated
in the days of the mule and cart. Some of the students took down
this oral testimony by hand, others tape-recorded and transcribed
the material. Not only did the students do extensive interviewing, but
they methodically searched community newspapers from 1900 to the
present to glean every bit of information about tobacco in the county.
They also collected old photographs of relevance to their study of the
tobacco industry.

The Skewarkians' next project was a slide-tape show of historical
places in Martin County, and from that experience they went on to a
forty-five-minute color super-8 movie based on the history and culture of the Tuscarora Indians in eastern North Carolina. Research on
this project resulted in many friendships between the students and
the Indians, who became more interested in their own heritage as
a result. Fresh from this experience with super-8 film production
(and moving into the "believe it or not" category!), students then
researched, wrote, and produced a ninety-five-minute super-8 film
based on the Civil War in Martin County, which included actual battle reenactments.

A significant part of the success of the Skewarkians is related to
the strong support of the school's principal, the district superintendent, and the parents. It was the parents, through the PTA, who pur-
chased the super-8 movie camera for the project. Recently, the
Skewarkians have received a National Endowment for the Humanities
Youth Grant to research and document the Roanoke River and its
importance, both past and present, to the local economy. Not content

with that, they are also busy collecting local folklore and ghost stories for possible publication, as well as doing research on the history of bootlegging in their home county.

On top of the Youth Grant and an initial gift of $1,300 from the school board to print the first edition of *Smoke to Gold* (which has subsequently more than paid for itself), the Skewarkians have raised money through selling doughnuts and magazine subscriptions.

When asked for advice for other teachers about to embark on similar projects, Elizabeth Roberson said, "Take one step at a time, otherwise it is overwhelming." For Roberson, the study of oral history is the logical place to begin in the struggle to make history relevant. "It is very difficult for a young person to imagine historical personages in the role of human beings who lived, breathed, and faced the same problems facing people today. A good social studies program, based on local history, will help bridge the gap with the past."

American Roots: Oral History as Theater

Located in Boston, the American Roots program successfully combined oral history and theater in an experimental approach to the study of immigration and migration in twentieth-century American history.[4] The program and its resultant theater production, "Yesterday, Today, and Tomorrow: Melting Pot, U.S.A.," was a product of the combined efforts of students, teachers, and parents from Winchester and Copeley Square High Schools and Theater Workshop Boston. Students worked intensively in small, multiethnic groups, collecting information from families and friends through oral history interviewing, and then created a theater piece that made a statement about life as experienced by different ethnic groups in Boston.

In the following passage, Daena Giadella of Theater Workshop Boston describes the purposes of the project and the ways in which, as she says, "memories were shaped into theater." "A significant and interesting part of the American Roots program was the interview process in which students had the opportunity to collect information about their ethnic roots from family members and friends. Each student was asked to conduct at least four interviews; some formulated their own questions and format, while others utilized an interview outline which we provided. In all cases, students were encouraged to be flexible, to allow the natural flow of communication to develop, to avoid feeling bound by specific questions and goals. It was soon found that these personal accounts of family background shed new light on everybody's awareness of various historical periods. Many humorous anecdotes were shared with the group.

One girl was surprised to find that the same 'facts' about life in the past were recalled in entirely different ways by different family members. In general, the interviews provided students with the chance for sharing with each other, while at the same time becoming active participants in the recording of their own history." The interviewing served to provide rich material for the translation of oral history into tangible dramatic form—an idea for a scene, a song, or a character—as the oral history data were transformed into the play, "Yesterday, Today, and Tomorrow: Melting Pot, U.S.A."

According to Giadella, "A major connecting point of theater and history can be seen in the realm of stories. History comes alive through theater, theater becomes relevant through history." In "Yesterday, Today, and Tomorrow," many stories from oral tradition were woven together. Some scenes in the play were based on the plot of a real-life incident described during the interviewing. In other instances, students extracted the essence of real ancestral characters and placed them in hypothetical situations where they might have encountered one another. The results were believable scenes that reflected the personal heritage of the students as well as pertinent social history of the early 1900s.

As the project went on, students were also asked to interview people from other ethnic groups than their own in order to obtain new insights and ideas for a scene dealing with ethnic stereotypes. The informants shared many anecdotes relating to experience with ethnic prejudice. With the help of staff members, students worked this material into a stage scene dealing with stereotypes, which showed "people statues" being moulded and released from ethnic slurs. The scene was particularly interesting because it gave students and audience a chance to identify with the pride and strengths of other ethnic groups.

The great range of ethnic backgrounds among students was revealed in a discussion seminar at the end of the project, when participants found no fewer than twenty-three different ethnicities to be represented. The process of oral history was basic to students' exploration of their own ethnic origins, to those of others, and to the creation of "Yesterday, Today, and Tomorrow."

The Great Depression: Hypotheses Testing

At Einstein High School, Montgomery County, Maryland, teacher Lois Martin found oral history to be a valid approach to researching the local effects of the Great Depression.[5]

The project began with a close study of the textbook analysis of the causes and effects of the Depression. Then students went on to read excerpts from firsthand accounts of the 1930s and to examine various historical interpretations of the Depression years. Finally, at the end of these preliminary studies, the class held a general discussion about the possible effects of the Depression upon the local community. They practiced turning these conjectures about local effects into clearly stated hypotheses, subject to testing by oral history research.

By this time Martin assumed that students had the general idea, and the class was broken up into research teams of four to six students. Each of these groups was given the specific task of coming up with a hypothesis that group members would investigate through interviews with local people who had lived through the Depression years.

Among the hypotheses formulated by the class were the following: "During the Depression most people lacked hope for the future." "The Depression caused people to become more dependent on government, thus losing their freedom." "Because of the Depression, many people lost faith in the stock market and became permanently thrifty." "The Depression severely affected very few people." "Because people blamed the Depression on the Republicans, most people alive then now vote for the Democrats." "During the Depression people felt threatened by an increase in crime." "During the Depression people had to work very hard." "People economized on clothing and weren't interested in fashion during the Depression." "There was a smaller generation gap than there is today." "People who lived during the Depression think young people today are spoiled." "People who lived through the Depression favor more government programs because they have seen what they can do." "The Depression changed people's morals—it made them more willing to help others and more conservative in personal behavior."

After formulating its specific hypothesis, each research team drew up a list of interview questions that would allow a tentative conclusion to be reached about the hypothesis. As the groups worked on their questions, they often came to realize that their original hypotheses needed restatement and refinement, or needed to have their terms operationally defined. For example, the students proposing to test the relative absence of a generation gap during the Depression found that they needed to define what generation gap really meant, and to decide on testable indicators of its presence or absence in local society. They ultimately concluded that a generation gap exists when adults and teenagers do not agree on, or work toward, common goals; when teenagers act without their parents' consent; and when teenagers believe that adults do not understand current conditions and, therefore, do not rely on adults for guidance. Questions designed to determine the extent of a generation gap would deal with adult-teenager community activities, parent-teenager cooperation at home, decisions parents make unilaterally for teenagers, decisions teenagers make unilaterally, and sources of adult-teenager disagreement, among others.

Each of the student research teams went through this process of hypothesis refinement, definition of terms, and questionnaire design, and the teams themselves decided how ambitious their interview schedules were to be. In some teams, students interviewed only one person, but other teams assigned each team member as many as five or six interviewees. Teams were also on their own to decide on appropriate kinds of informants (age, sex, income group, etc.) to use for testing their hypothesis, to locate suitable interviewees within these categories, and to conduct structured interviews using the questionnaire they had designed. All recognized that in no cases would teams be able to interview enough persons to decisively support or reject their hypotheses, but fascinating new data could be obtained.

Each team member wrote up his or her interview (or interviews), analyzed its support or lack of support for the team hypothesis, and compared the information gathered orally to that previously read, heard, or viewed on film. The research teams then presented group reports to the class about the results of their research.

The period of research team reports and subsequent group discussion of the reports went on for several days. Students had discovered many fascinating things about the local effects—and, in some cases, the lack of effects—of the Great Depression. They learned of the variety of strategies local people had used just to get by during the 1930s. They heard a wide spectrum of emotional opinion about FDR and the programs of his New Deal. And they found some informants who had the Depression and World War II, the 1930s and the 1940s, all mixed up in their minds—food stamps and the WPA, Hoover and Hitler!

In general, however, local realities seemed more complicated than the cut-and-dried explanations of the textbook. Some local persons had actually prospered during the Depression years; others reported only a few hardships, while yet others had suffered terribly from its effects. Informants who had moved to the community from other localities since the 1930s also had very different stories to tell. Regarding the hypothesis about a general increase of crime during the Depression, a person who had come from the small-town Midwest reported that: "Nobody was afraid to go out at night. There was no crime at all." But a former southerner told a different story: "Crime was extremely high—robbery, moonshining—people carried guns. Even my grandfather carried a gun, and he was a preacher."

In the team reports, unemployment during the Depression was described by students with a vividness possible only because they talked to the people to whom it really happened. "When the mine that my grandfather was working at closed, the family's income ceased completely," one boy related. "No money was coming in so they had to provide for themselves. They farmed what land they had for vegetables, and they got milk from their cow. Their meat was supplied by a few pigs and their hunting skill. Since they could not afford bullets for the guns, they had to find where the groundhogs were and dig them up."

Teacher Lois Martin's final analysis of her project was highly positive. She concluded that the same general approach might be used to investigate the local impact of World War II, the Korean War, Vietnam, or the civil rights movement. As she summed things up, "formulating hypotheses, writing questions, and analyzing interviews is group work at its finest. Everyone is needed; everyone must participate. The bookish, and those who are not, both contribute. The final presentation cannot be engineered by one or two students alone, since interpretations must be in depth and the analysis must be both imaginative and valid."

Who Are You? We Are Italo-Americans

At Woburn High School, Woburn, Massachusetts, language teacher Shirley Anne Wilson concluded that "in a community where twenty-six percent of the population is Italo-American, living in an extended family situation, a purely academic approach to the Italian language would not be appropriate. There had to be a better way to integrate community resources, the students' own experiences, and the high school curriculum." Wilson wanted her students to practice aural-oral skills and to review grammar, vocabulary, and composition, but she felt that this was just not enough. Something was missing.

The answer came to Wilson in the summer of 1978 when she was reading a history book written in the form of first-person accounts. Oral history was the method for which she had been searching.[6] As she tells it, "What better way to teach appreciation of ethnic heritage and cultural pluralism, while at the same time reviewing basic skills, than to have students interview their own grandparents?"

The efforts of Shirley Anne Wilson and fifteen of her language students resulted in a book anthology of life histories entitled *Who Are You? We Are Italo-Americans*. In the beginning, students studied and practiced the procedures of oral history, discussed possible research topics in class, and did preliminary reading about the history of Woburn since the turn of the century. Then, equipped with tape recorders, note pads, and a solid measure of enthusiasm, the students began a ten-week research project in the Woburn Italian community. The assignment included the students interviewing their grandparents in Italian, transcribing the interviews in Italian, and then translating the results into English. The interview topics included the experience of immigration, problems of adjusting to life in the United States, life experiences during the Depression, coping with World Wars I and II, and changes in the political, social, and educational aspects of the city of Woburn.

Community support for the project was high, and a great deal of technical Italian was learned in the process of researching, transcribing, translating, and editing the book. In the end, Wilson was firmly convinced that the project had promoted better communication and understanding between the generations, enabling her students to gain a richer sense of their own identities. After the project, history, language learning, sociology, and economics no longer seemed esoteric areas of study. Learning had been relevant, direct, and personal. As one student fieldworker put it, "After all my grandfather went through, I don't feel right doing nothing with my life."

Loblolly: A Descendent of *Foxfire*

As previously noted, the *Foxfire* example has spawned over two hundred student oral history magazines across the United States. One of the earliest of these descendants of *Foxfire* was *Loblolly*, a magazine produced at Gary High School in east Texas. After nine years and over thirty sixty-four page issues, the *Loblolly* journal is still going strong; its history can stand for the experiences of many other *Foxfire* descendants.[7]

Originally from Maine, teacher Lincoln King came to rural east Texas after obtaining a degree in the classics from Brown University and pursuing an early career in the aerospace industry. As he told us in a 1977 interview, "I had taught at Gary a year and a half when at Christmas of 1972 my wife got a copy of the first *Foxfire* book. I grabbed the book and went all the way through it over Christmas vacation. As I read, I thought that, if these kids can do it, Texas kids can do it. So, after vacation was over in January 1973, I went back out to school and I got tentative clearances. Nobody, including myself, knew exactly what we were trying to do."

King and his social studies and journalism classes soon found out. The Gary students were impressed by the stories in *The Foxfire Book* and agreed with King that if rural Georgia could do this, rural Texas could do it too. Like King himself, they had no previous training or experience in oral history, but were willing to learn.

The first problem was money, and *The Foxfire Book*, though offering good examples of the kind of research articles that were possible, offered no information on this crucial matter. The Gary school gave them the go-ahead but offered no funding. So, to get started, the project sold stock in its unresearched and yet-to-be-published oral history journal.

"We sold stock to parents, relatives, and businesses for $2 a share. If you bought one share of stock, you got a free copy of the first issue of the magazine. If you bought five shares, you got a year's subscription. They didn't know what they were buying, and we didn't know what we were selling."

With the stock sales money, the *Loblolly* project bought their first tape recorder for cash and made a down payment on an IBM Selectric typewriter. Arrangements were made to use the school's yearbook camera. The stock funds stretched just far enough to pay for the magazine's first issue, a publishing cost of $350. Whatever the stock purchasers may have thought they were paying for, they were pleased with the final product. The first issue of *Loblolly* quickly sold out, and King and his students were delighted to find that they suddenly had more than enough cash in hand for *Loblolly*, volume 1, number 2.

Almost a decade later, the *Loblolly* journal (named for the native loblolly pine tree) is still a going concern; for King and his successive generations of high school students, the process still works. *Loblolly* students have done many articles on the traditional history, folklore, and folk crafts of their native east Texas. They have interviewed retired sheriffs, farmers, mill workers, and rural craftspersons of all kinds. The magazine has been discussed in *Newsweek* and a score of other journals and newspapers. Lincoln King and his students have traveled widely, both in Texas and elsewhere, presenting their account of the *Loblolly* experience to interested audiences. The project is a strong, viable program, producing a magazine whose readership now extends far beyond east Texas.

But the basic pattern of *Loblolly* remains unaltered from 1973. The oral history enterprise is still exciting, and the journalistic products of that research are still deeply appreciated by the local community. Teacher Lincoln King summed it all up very well at the end of the 1977 interview, and we will let him tell it.

> The kids are a lot more involved than in the normal school process; they are involved in decision making. At first, I had to almost shake the kids; they are conditioned just like the rest of us. They sit in school waiting for someone to tell them what to do. All of a sudden someone comes along and says "What do you think about this?" They developed a lot of self confidence as they made decisions . . .
>
> There is a product involved—something tangible and visible. It's been tremendously rewarding for me and rewarding for them to be able to see the fruits of their efforts appear in print. So much of what students do in school is intangible and unrecognized. Often, only two people see it, the student and the teacher. When they produce something that is seen by hundreds of people it's gratifying but it's motivating too.
>
> What we've been trying to do with the magazine is to discover, collect, and preserve local and regional history of East Texas. While the students are doing this, they discover much, much more about themselves, their own roots, culture and heritage. A lot of times they talk to members of their family for the first time ever. Some of them discover that parents and grandparents didn't always have grey hair. It's also been great for the people they talked to. A lot of times older people feel ignored or forgotten. Then, for perhaps the first time, somebody is interested in something that they are doing or that they have done. It's a little bit of immortality, I guess.
>
> It's also been good for the school. Schools can use good public relations. So, it's been good for the school and for the community.
>
> What is, I suppose, most important to me is the human impact of *Loblolly*. What is important is what happened to everybody involved with us—the students who do the work on the project, the people they talk to, and all the people who are touched by the project in various ways. It affects us all. It changes us.

Lagniappe, or "Something Extra"

How far down the grade levels will oral history work? Probably a good bit farther than many would think. *Lagniappe*, a biannual oral history magazine published by fourth graders at the Chamberline Elementary School in West Baton Rouge, Louisiana, is now in its third year. The word *lagniappe* is an old Louisiana French term meaning "something extra"—something above and beyond the usual or the ordinary. The description certainly fits.[8]

Teacher Tom Arceneaux, whose classes are made up of rural blacks and French Arcadians, saw the project as a way to record the passing of a way of life, as well as to provide an inspiration to the younger generations to value and continue some of those cultural traditions. Although Arceneaux and his students spend many recesses and after-school hours on magazine work, *Lagniappe* basically comes out of one self-contained classroom. In 1977–78, the project received the support of an ESEA Title IV-C Teacher Incentive Grant that allowed *Lagniappe* to buy additional tape recorders, tapes, and 35 mm slide film. Arceneaux wherever possible attempts to incorporate magazine work into the formal curriculum, and feels strongly about the basic skills that are acquired through the project. As he describes the process, "The kids learn how to get the main idea from the interviews and then to rewrite them into their own words. Because I require them to turn in articles handwritten in ink, neatness and correct letter formation become important. In addition, in learning how to interview they learn how to interact with and be sensitive to the many different people they come in contact with."

In a 1978 article about the *Lagniappe* project in *Childhood Education*, Tom Arceneaux was optimistic about the possibilities for other oral history projects in elementary school classrooms. "*Your* community is also filled with unwritten lore. Elementary school pupils are just as capable of collecting it as are high schoolers. If your class is showing signs of apathy and indifference from too heavy an emphasis on textbook history, why not give them a chance to write their own? Besides becoming involved with important older people, they can learn to observe carefully and accurately, contribute to the preservation of local values and wisdom—and have a very good time to boot!"

The South Boston Project: Oral History of an Urban Neighborhood

Classroom oral history does not have to be a rural and small town phenomenon; it can work in the inner city as well. That is what South Boston High School teacher Deborah Insell concluded after reading *The Foxfire Book*, and subsequent events have proved her correct in her judgment. Insell saw the core idea as simple and adaptable; it was "students learning from elders" and, as she said, "It worked so well for the *Foxfire* students that I wanted to try it for myself." Then Insell and her English students at South Boston High went on to show that the idea worked for them also.[9]

The project they chose was an oral history of the South Boston neighborhood. The last such history had been published in 1901, and because the neighborhood was profoundly ethnic (and very proud of it), an oral history seemed a sound way to unite young and old in a worthwhile project. It fulfilled the need for a "subject in which both the students and the elderly had an intense interest, so that both groups feel as though they were working toward a common goal." The South Boston history would not be "merely of important events and famous people" (like many places South Boston was short on these) but a social history of the home neighborhood from 1900 to the present.

Eight weeks prior to beginning the project, Insell began attending senior citizen meetings, talking to people, getting the names of others to call, and in general trying to recruit elderly persons who would contribute their time and information. She also put articles about the project in the local paper and recruited the advice and assistance of the local librarian, who was also an active community historian. In the end, she found a healthy number of elderly South Bostonians who volunteered to be interviewed for the project.

"Writing Our Own History of South Boston" was a seven-week elective English course in which thirty-five students and twenty-five elders took part. The first two weeks were a crash course in oral history interviewing covering the usual range of practical subjects. In the third week, students chose topics from a general list, designed questions to explore the chosen topics, and began to conduct interviews. The general topics covered by the South Boston study of community social history were family life, houses and neighborhoods, schools, community control, work, leisure time, religious life, obsolete institutions, relationships to national events, and eminent persons.

Interviewing went on for the next three weeks. Under the usual procedure, a group of three or four students working on a chosen topic would interview an informant for about forty-five minutes somewhere on the school premises. Insell noted that "On some days there would be three or four separate interviews going on during the students' class in different nooks and cubbyholes of our crowded school." On days when a research team was not interviewing, it would be listening to its tapes and taking notes. Each group was to have at least four interviews from which to write its particular section of the history.

In the last two weeks of the course, the students wrote, revised, corrected, and finally handed in their section of the history to the student editors. The student editors then prepared the book for typing. Later, *The History of South Boston: 1900 to the Present* was presented to the Boston Bicentennial Committee at a tea in honor of the elderly participants, and the tapes were placed in the local library for permanent community use. In a course evaluation completed at the end of the seven-week project, Insell's students were overwhelmingly positive about the value of the course. Attitudes toward history, their community, and its older citizens had all changed, and changed for the better.

A Typology of Project Options

We hope that these examples suggest something of the range of potential applications for classroom oral history, as well as something of its excitement for students and teachers. In the following section we go beyond the case studies to offer a typology of project options, a grab-bag of classroom project ideas in oral history. The ideas come from the literature, from ERIC microfiche, from personal contacts with teachers, and from our own experiences and imaginations. But before we begin, we would like to make several introductory points about these project ideas in oral history.

1. The suggested ideas are both practical and imaginative, real and imagined. Many of the projects mentioned come from the literature of classroom oral history. Others are entirely our own, extrapolated from what has been done, and from what (we deeply suspect) teachers somewhere are already doing. Feel free to take them with a grain of salt. But the job of our ideas chapter is to think big—to help would-be practitioners of oral history to "prime the pump" and come up with their own projects.

2. These project suggestions follow a principle of "splitting" rather than "lumping." To help illustrate the range of classroom oral history, we have particularized ideas rather than grouped them together. There are, for example, several different versions of the family oral history project and several variations of the project in folklore. We could have lumped these under two general discussions, but, for the purposes of this ideas chapter, we chose to discuss them in their several variations.

3. These project ideas are interdisciplinary and multigrade in their potential application, and we avoid saying exactly how and where we think they may be applied. Once again, as the preceding case studies have emphasized, this is because classroom oral history

has proven adaptable for subjects from history to home economics, and from grade levels from high elementary to college. Our typology of project options explores classroom ideas appropriate for history and the social studies, but other kinds of project ideas are included, and many of the projects described are of a general nature, adaptable to several disciplines.

For example, a life history interview with an elderly weaver of white-oak baskets is a project appropriate for history, English, home economics, or vocational arts; the differences between these would be a matter of disciplinary perspective and emphasis, not of substance. From a historical perspective, this might be a study of an early craft and craftsperson of economic importance in community life. For English, it might be an oral autobiography, a work of oral literature. For home economics and vocational arts, the life history interview would be a procedure for documenting and preserving a valuable folk craft of potential interest and usefulness to students and others in the present-day community.

To us, each of these subject-area approaches to this particular example of oral life history seems almost equally appropriate. The way the idea is applied, and at what level of scale and complexity, must be a matter for the teacher to decide. We would not presume to do this, nor do we presume to tell teachers which ideas are appropriate to what grade levels. The oral life history (to return to that example) can be as simple as a student recording a single interview with a grandparent and then bringing the tape to class for others to share. But it can be as ambitious as Theodore Rosengarten's study of Nate Shaw—hundreds of interview hours, thousands of transcript pages, and a book!

It probably won't be that ambitious, of course, but our point is that both these projects, the twenty-minute tape and the six-hundred-page book, are valid applications of the oral life history idea. The first is, perhaps, appropriate for the fourth grade and the second for the graduate school.

Other project ideas offer the same interdisciplinary and multi-grade options. The task of adapting the projects suggested below to subject, grade level, and school circumstances must and should be left up to the classroom teacher. In the real world of schools and classrooms it could scarcely be otherwise. In expectation of this, the ideas in the typology of project options are given a general description only, with detailed application the job of the teacher. And what if these project ideas stimulate teachers to devise other and completely different ones? Well, they will have done their job even better.

An Oral Autobiography
Students tape-record their own oral life history interview about their lives to date, from earliest memories to the present.

As in the case of many of the subsequent ideas, this project can be as modest or ambitious as circumstances merit. Students might research their early life by talking informally to parents, grand-parents, siblings, and other relatives. They might examine whatever documentation their personal histories have accumulated up to this point—birth certificates, early school work, parents' diaries and per-sonal letters, etc.—for possible incorporation into their autobiogra-phy. But most of all, students should search their memories about their own life experiences.

They are likely to find this a fascinating process. All of us can remember much more about our lives than we may initially believe, and students should persevere in their introspection, jotting down memories as they occur. This kind of research works best if the pro-cess of remembering and the process of writing become closely linked. During the introspection period of the project, students should formulate questions to ask themselves about their personal histories, such as: What are my very earliest memories? (And why those memories, and not others?) What sorts of things did I like to do as a baby? As a small child? What sorts of activities often got me into trouble? Was there anything I was forbidden to do as a child? Were there places I wasn't allowed to go? What were my greatest child-hood fears? What do I remember about the day I first went to school? What were the stand-out events (teachers, incidents, and the like) of my early school days? The process can go on and on. As it does, students will discover that the formulation of appropriate questions to ask themselves can play a powerful role in helping them recall their past lives—a very important lesson to remember when they go on to interview others.

After students have interviewed parents, grandparents, and sib-lings about their lives and carried the process of introspection as far as they reasonably can, they get ready to create their oral autobiogra-phy. First, they look back through their notes and begin to arrange them in a rough chronological order; they are, in effect, putting to-gether the topical script that they will use when they narrate their autobiography. After students have decided what they plan to talk about—the chronology, the topics, the sequencing, etc.—they simply use the cassette tape recorder to tell the story of their lives in their own words. This is done in one session, or in as many sessions as they prefer, stopping or starting the tape recorder when they wish.

The oral autobiography is informal, a "talk-through" of their life histories to the tape recorder. But before students finish the project, they will have learned a great deal about research, oral history, the way the long-term memory works, and perhaps themselves as well.

Living History: Classroom Interviews of Community Informants
Students locate community people (e.g., a blacksmith, an early doctor) with unique life experiences, special skills, areas of expertise, and other valuable firsthand knowledge about the community past, and invite them to a classroom interview.

The living history project is an exploration of local history through direct, face-to-face interaction with the persons who lived it. Students might recruit these resource persons from among their own relatives and acquaintances. A list might be compiled of community persons willing to come to the classroom, along with the frequency with which they would be able to attend and their special area of historical knowledge or expertise. (And please note that area of historical expertise may be of more than local relevance; it may relate to national and international events as well.)

In any case, each visit should include the following sequence: (1) The teacher and students decide on a topic or topics of general relevance. (2) Students locate a person or persons knowledgeable about the chosen topic and willing to come to the classroom to be interviewed. (3) Then, students do preliminary research on the topic of the interview; they informally interview parents and grandparents about it and do background readings if printed information is available. (4) After this period of preliminary research, students discuss and develop appropriate questions to ask the informants during the classroom interview. The class should do the interviewees the courtesy of being soundly prepared, so far as this is possible, about the topic under study. (5) The resource people visit the classroom and are interviewed. Several formats are possible for this, but it will probably be best to let the informants talk about the topic on their own for several minutes. Many of the class's prepared questions will doubtless be answered as they go along. Questions they did not answer, and additional questions suggested by their statements, may then be brought up. (6) Finally, after the resource people have gone, the class engages in a postvisit debriefing of the interview. This critical stage should not be neglected, because it is the chance for the class to analyze the informants' testimony as "historical truth."

If at all possible, interviews should be taped for future reference and classroom use. The students should remember that the visitors are doing the class a big favor, and they should try to ensure that the interview setting is as friendly, low-key, and informal as possible. The resource people should be treated in such a way as to make them even more willing to return to this or another classroom.

An Oral History of the Home Neighborhood

Working alone or in research teams, students collect oral history data for a study of their home neighborhoods.

This could be the study of a complete neighborhood or of some segment of one, such as a block or a street. The object is to find out how the neighborhood has developed and changed across time, as perceived by long-term residents. Students decide upon the topical and chronological limits of their study, formulate a set of general questions with which to begin their interviews, and then go out into the community to locate suitable informants. As in the South Boston case study discussed earlier in the chapter, students in urban areas are likely to find a strong sense of neighborhood identity and loyalty—to learn that, for many older urbanites, neighborhood membership seems to mean more than membership in the city as a whole. Possible topics to explore in the interviews include the ultimate origins of the neighborhood (did the neighborhood originate in a separate suburb or small town, and then become incorporated?), the economic rise or fall of the neighborhood, ethnic and socioeconomic changes in the neighborhood over the decades, and present problems and prospects for the future. Student researchers should take their lead in part from the neighborhood residents themselves; a preliminary interview or two may well suggest significant directions to pursue. The neighborhood council (if one exists) and other neighborhood groups are likely to be very interested in what the students are doing and quite helpful in locating good interviewees.

A Memory Book

Not all classroom oral history projects require tape recorders, and the memory book is a good case in point. Students brainstorm the questions to include in a memory book with which to interview one or both of their grandparents. The question design process could be part of a home assignment, could go on during class discussion, or could be a combination of the two. The idea is to come up with a series of good questions for inclusion in the memory book, with space allowed for the students to write down their grandparents' answers. The book then becomes a significant remembrance of their grandparents to be preserved down through the years. The memory book project is perhaps more appropriate for the high elementary through junior high grades, but, once again, the general idea is subject to different levels of application. Some questions younger students might ask are: What sorts of games did you play when you were a kid? What kind of school did you attend? Students should agree on some thirty to fifty questions to ask, most requiring relatively short answers. Then the questions could be typed, leaving sufficient space for students to write in the answers. The sheets can be photocopied or otherwise duplicated to allow a memory book for each student. Students can take the book with them and interview their chosen grandparents—learning something about oral history and creating a significant memento of their personal history.

Researching the Origins of Local Place Names
Using a topographic map of the home county as a basic reference, students use the oral history to discover the origins of local place names and learn the history of their area. These names would be those of communities, roads, city streets, streams, hills, and other natural and artificial features. The teacher might post a topographic map of the county area under study, and students could research the origins of place names on the map by asking other students, teachers, parents, grandparents, and other persons who might know the origin of the name. A given project might choose to concentrate on any of the several place-name categories—city streets, rivers and creeks, rural communities, etc. Students should be alert for older place names for streets and communities now known by another name (for example, the hamlet of Webberville in rural Travis County, Texas, was once called Hog Eye!). Students might undertake individual projects in place-name origins in the areas closest to their homes, or the whole class might work on a single place name at the same time, collecting and analyzing the various explanations of its origin.

In fact, students are likely to find that they must choose between alternative explanations of the origins of many place names in the locality. They will have to weigh such factors as the age of the informant, the numbers of informants giving the same theory of origin, the plausibility and internal consistency of the various explanations, and the degree to which these explanations square with what is known about the history of the area. These are precisely the sort of questions with which the practicing historian must grapple, and place-name research is an excellent introduction to the field.

As research progresses, explanations of place-name origins

could be keyed by numbers to the posted topographic map, and this annotated map might stay with the teacher as a permanent resource in local history. (Here, as elsewhere, students and teacher should not overlook the research possibilities suggested by the telephone.)

An Oral History of the School

Assuming that your school is not "shiny-new," students might embark on a project to write its "official" history. Because many of the most interesting aspects of school life never show up in the documents, oral history seems an appropriate way to go about this. Students could research school records, old newspapers from school and community, and the memories of past students, teachers, and administrators. Extensive interviews should be conducted with these former inmates, and students should not neglect to talk to former secretaries and building custodians, who sometimes know more than anybody else about the inner workings of the school.[10]

The finished history could take a variety of forms, including a more or less chronological account of major developments in the life of the school (new wings added, state championship football teams, etc.); a social history of the school through the years (student and faculty dress and demeanor, student pastimes, clubs, etc.); or a series of oral history interviews with earlier students, teachers, and administrators, transcribed and published verbatim.

Many of the interviews for the school project might be conducted right on the school premises, and would give good experience to students in preparation for other institutional oral histories in the community—churches, clubs, and the like.

Oral Histories of Local Buildings

Approaching local buildings as historical "problems," students can use both documentary and oral sources to research their histories. The building under study could be an old home, a commercial structure downtown, a church, an old industrial site, etc. Students would search city records and interview past owners or occupants of the building to answer a series of historical questions about it. For example, who built the structure? When was it built? Who has lived in it or used it? What activities have gone on there over the years? What modifications (internal or external) have been made to the structure? What significant events, if any, have gone on in and around it? Does the structure play a role in community folklore—are stories told about it? (Is it, for example, "haunted"?) Many other questions are possible, and the old building provides a natural focus for the student oral history project. Students might work on a building alone or in research teams of four or five. In any case, they are likely to unearth some fascinating stories.

The Oral Life History: General
Some aspects of the oral life history project are examined in chapter 1. In the oral life history, students tape-record interviews with elderly persons, then transcribe and edit those interviews into coherent narratives, in which the informants tell their own stories in their own words. Students are much more than just passive recorders in this process, because the oral life history is an interactive product of *both* interviewee and interviewer. Students' creativity, social sensitivity, and linguistic skills are critical to the success of the interviews and the transcription and editing process that follows.[11]

In the general form of the oral life history the student is concerned with recording the entire life story of the informant, from earliest childhood memories to the present. The general procedure for the oral life history takes place in four sequential stages: (1) locating a suitable informant; (2) conducting the initial interview; (3) analyzing the tape, self-correction, and conducting follow-up interviews; and (4) transcribing and editing.

The human life forms a natural focus for oral history research, and students will find that good subjects are close at hand. In fact, an elderly person from the students' own family or circle of close family friends is often the ideal. Many students initially will be more comfortable interviewing a grandmother or a great aunt than a perfect stranger, and they can approach their interviews with a body of basic knowledge about the personalities and life experiences of their informants. Likewise, the subjects will be more at ease in the interview setting and are more likely to regard the whole procedure as highly appropriate—an oral transmission of family traditional history across the generations. That this process is intended to produce a tangible "something" in the form of the transcribed life history adds to the perceived worth of the enterprise.

But good subjects may come from anywhere. Students should remember the case of Nate Shaw! Almost invariably, the informants' initial reluctance, shyness, or suspicion can be overcome by the interview process itself, because the oral life history interview is profoundly flattering to its subjects, and they are almost certain to warm to the task. The initial "Why me?" stage does not last very long for any elderly person with a healthy ego; the question soon becomes "When are you going to come back?" or perhaps even "What kept you?"

Additional aspects of the oral life history will be explored in later chapters, but here the following points may be made: (1) unlike some other project options, the oral life history is a prototype idea, of which many of the other projects are but specialized applications; (2) the full-scale oral life history is an extensive project, always requiring several interviews to complete; and (3) during the interview process the informant *must* feel free to "skip around" in his or her life story— to follow whatever associations come up. Even when the interviewer is very experienced, the life history interview and re-interview rarely follow a strictly chronological sequence, beginning with earliest memories and ending with the present. The long-term memory just does not seem to work that way. The informant must feel free to "circle back" to earlier periods or topics as additional material about them is recalled. In the course of several interviews, this circling process greatly increases the body of information on any given chronological period or topic.

The oral life history project may result only in a series of tapes. Alternatively, the tapes may be completely or selectively transcribed and the transcripts edited into a coherent narrative, chronologically arranged—the oral life history proper. Again, the scale and sophistication with which the idea is applied may vary greatly.

The Oral Life History: Topical Focus

The topical oral life history is simply a more limited variation of the general project. Unlike the general life history, it has a topical focus, which is explored throughout the life story of the informant. The topical focus could come from classroom discussion and/or the student interviewer, or it could be a natural focus, discerned from the informant's preoccupations in an exploratory first interview. In either case, interview topics may be quite varied: a grandfather's life as a farmer (or a banker, or a mill worker, etc.); a grandmother's career as a homemaker and her attitudes about that role; or an elderly citizen's experiences with and attitudes toward local, state, and national governments and the role they have played in his life. Many other topical emphases are possible.

The Oral Life History: Chronological Focus

The chronological focus is another more limited version of the general oral life history. In this variation, the interviewer is concerned to elicit a detailed account (on a wide range of topics) of a certain period in the informant's life—his or her childhood, school years, courtship and marriage, or life since retirement. As in the case of the topically focused oral life history, this emphasis may come from the classroom or be discerned from a natural emphasis present in a first, exploratory interview. Many informants will be found to stress one period of their life over others, and the study may choose to follow that lead. The chronological focus is another way of limiting the oral life history and keeping it to a manageable scale. It also allows student researchers to deal with more than one informant. For example, in a project focused on "growing up fifty years ago," the student would probably have the opportunity to interview several persons about their early childhood memories and experiences.[12]

The Oral Life History: Student

The oral life history project does not have to focus on the lives of the elderly; it can involve students in interviews with their peers or with students younger than themselves. Class members might pair up to interview each other about their lives to date, or they could interview younger children about their lives (siblings? cousins?). This raises some very interesting questions: What do children remember about their childhood when they are still children? Is their knowledge different from and/or more detailed than later, after adult experience has intervened? It might be enlightening to find out.

The Oral Life History: Folk/Popular Artist

This last variant of the oral life history project studies both the life experience and the "verbal art" of some folk or popular artist in the community—a poet, a songwriter, a folk or popular musician, etc. In this study, both the artist and his or her art are subjects for analysis. (The model for this project idea, which cannot be discussed in detail here, is B. Lee Cooper's "Oral History, Popular Music, and Les Mc-Cann" in *The Social Studies*.)[13]

Family Life Histories

Growing up within the web of biological and cultural interrelationships of the human family is the universal experience of almost all persons, and an appropriate place for oral history to begin. In the historical quest for who you are, the most basic questions are to be answered closest to home, among one's parents, grandparents, and other family members. Not so long ago, much of the oral traditional history of the family was transmitted informally, from older to younger, sitting around the fire or on the front porch. Today, life is faster and more disjointed, the generation gap is wider, and there are fewer opportunities for the transmission of family traditions. The family oral history project, however, is one way to encourage this transmission process to continue.

The first of several variants of family oral history is the family life history project, in which students interview several family members about their lives. In a sense, this project is a composite form of the topical oral life history idea. The topical focus of the interviews is the family itself, its career across time, and the role of the various interviewees within it. The family itself is the link—the topic—that ties this series of life history interviews together. Family members are invited to discuss their own lives in relationship to the family, to recount family anecdotes and traditions (old stories handed down across the generations), and to discuss socioeconomic and cultural changes in the family across time. Students' project tapes might become the basis of a class report (written or oral), or could become part of some more ambitious presentation on the history of their family (see below).

A Family Genealogy/Oral History Project
In this version of the family oral history project, students would combine genealogical research with oral history to link the living and the dead in their family histories. They could use the local genealogy library to trace one or both of their family lines back several generations. Then they could map this web of biological relationships on a genealogical chart. As any good genealogical manual would recommend, the documentary research might be combined with the interview of students' older living relations about family history, including names, relationships, and geographical movements of family members—important clues to guide the direction of a documentary search.

If no genealogical library is immediately available, this project could take the form of a preliminary oral history of family genealogy in preparation for the documentary search. Once again, this is how many genealogical researchers would recommend that you begin—glean all available evidence from the oral traditions of the family before turning to the genealogical library and the documents.[14]

A Family Archive Project
In this project, students serve as family archivists to discover, record, and inventory the written, visual, artifactual, and oral sources for their family histories. They search attics for old photographs and documents and interview older relatives to record oral testimony about family history. In the end these raw data for a comprehensive

family history may be gathered together in one collection or may simply be inventoried—listed and described. The inventory would include a description of the historical resource, who in the family has it, where it is located, and other relevant information. At the end of the inventory process, the student archivists will have summarized the documentary, photographic, and artifactual evidence about the history of their family, as well as created a series of oral history tapes recording the evidence preserved in living memory. Everything is ready for the family historian to do his or her job.

The Comprehensive Family History

The next, and most ambitious, student family history project would go beyond archiving the historical evidence to the actual creation of a comprehensive family history in a book-length format. Building on the work of the archival phase of family history research, the student would order all the different kinds of historical data into a coherent whole, tracing what is known about the family from earliest times to the present. Such a family story would begin with genealogy and end with oral history, incorporating the existing documentary evidence along the way, including deeds, diaries, wills, personal letters, and the like. To craft the family history, the student must practice, and to a degree master, the skills of genealogist, archivist, oral historian, and writer. It is a challenging project, but given sufficient time, energy, and motivation, teachers may be surprised at what students will be able to accomplish.

A Family Cookbook and Social History

This modest family history idea has more to it than might first appear, because traditional recipes are a significant part of family lore and a source of real pride to some family members. They are passed down through the generations, usually with anecdotes and stories illustrating their origins and the incidents and behaviors of family members closely associated with them and the occasions of their preparation. In short, family recipes are an "in" to family social history. In the family cookbook project students collect *both* the recipe itself and the context of social history that gives the recipe its meaning to the family. This includes the oral testimony about (1) the origins of the recipe and its line of transmission in the family; (2) any anecdotes about individual family members associated with the recipe; and (3) the historical and cultural significance of the recipe, including its association with special events, dates, or holidays in family history or its ethnic, cultural, or religious meanings to the ethnic, cultural, or religious groups of which the family is a part.

Exploring Family Roots

In another variant of family oral history (perhaps as an introduction to a more ambitious project), students might interview their oldest family members to collect family historical traditions of the greatest possible time depth. These would be the oldest traditions about the family and its origins, the stories told to students' grandparents by *their* grandparents. The idea is to discover and record oral traditions that go back as many generations as possible. These may be stories about what happened to the family on the way to its present location, stories about colorful ancestors, stories about Indians or about the Civil War. But the basic idea is to explore the ultimate limits of the family oral traditional history. ("Oral history" is orally transmitted recollections of events directly experienced by the informant; "oral traditional history" is orally transmitted recollections of events experienced by others.)

In any case, students should be optimistic about the possibilities. They should recall that for Alex Haley these earliest family traditions were words and phrases from a West African language and stories about an African—a time depth approaching two hundred years![15]

Family Oral History: A "Natural Context" Study

Students collect a variety of family traditions—stories, anecdotes about family members, incidents, and the like—as these are naturally recounted at family reunions and holidays. Folklorists usually distinguish between folklore collected in the "natural context," as it occurs naturally in the process of social interaction, and folklore collected in an "artificial context," in which the folklorist specifically requests for it to be performed. Most of the oral history project ideas in this chapter require artificial contexts, many in a formal interview setting with a tape recorder present. But in this study the tape recorder is dispensed with, and the student researcher simply "listens in" and waits for items of oral history to be performed in the natural context of family reunions and holidays—the times the family gathers together to renew present relationships and to relive the past. This kind of study of spontaneous oral history can tell us much about how people use oral traditions in their ongoing social relationships.

Historic Photographs and Oral History

In a project that might go on either inside or outside of the students' immediate families, students locate valuable historical photographs and use oral history to record the photo owners' explanations about the origins and historical contents of the photographs.[16]

Photographs, the visual evidence of history, are attracting a lot of attention these days from both historians and collectors. We are coming to realize that these "windows into time" offer a unique glimpse into the life of the past, a kind of glimpse that no verbal descriptions, documentary or oral, can provide.

This project would have the student (1) locate a certain number of historic photographs in the family attic or in the hands of others in the community; (2) conduct a brief oral history interview with the owners of the photos about their contents; (3) rephotograph (or photocopy) the photos for permanent record; and (4) bring photocopies and oral history tapes to class for purposes of display. Hence, students would have collected both the historic image and the context of oral recollection in which it is in a sense embedded. This context of oral history gives the photo much of its meaning.

Until very recently, historians have treated old photos rather like nineteenth-century archaeologists treated artifacts—ripping through their historical context to obtain them for purposes of display, often disregarding or even destroying the context in the process. This project may be in some sense an exercise, but in it students would operate on the cutting edge of historical procedures with regard to the visual document.

The Community at War

Perhaps no international event alters people's lives so profoundly as war, and this is almost as true for those who remain on the home front. Since 1914, Americans have fought in World War I, World War II, Korea, and Vietnam, and many veterans of those wars are to be found in the community. In the community at war project students locate combat veterans (or veterans of the home front) for a series of oral history interviews about community participation in war. Focus of the study could be one war or several, an emphasis upon actual combat experience or upon the experiences of persons who never saw actual combat, but whose lives were profoundly changed by it. Possible topics of study include (1) the community's experience in a single war (such as the case study of the Baton Rouge "Americans in Vietnam" project); (2) the changes in women's work—and family roles—during World War II; (3) differences in the experience of combat between World War II, Korea, and Vietnam; (4) differences in the attitudes of the several veterans' groups toward "their war"; and (5) possible changes in the way people *remember* war across time.

A Mainstreet Oral History
In this project, students interview the long-term owner-operators of downtown businesses about their professional careers, about changes they have observed in the downtown area over the decades, and about what they believe are current trends. The natural limits of this study are the geographic limits of the core business area or historic town center—the main commercial street, the town square, etc. Each interview would begin by recording the life career of the respective business owner (a kind of topical life history). Then, emphasis would shift to the individual's perceptions of historical changes on "Main Street": its economic rise and/or fall, ethnic shifts, the rise and fall of different sorts of businesses, changes in the socioeconomic status of customers, downswings or upswings in crime and violence, and attempts at historic restoration and downtown revitalization. Each business owner becomes the source of a new viewpoint of downtown: where it came from, what it is, and where it seems to be going.

An Oral History of a Local Industry
Students conduct an oral history of an important local industry such as lumbering, mining, or petrochemical refining—any industry economically significant to the home community. To chronicle the human side of its development, they interview workers and management, past and present, about the way the industry has affected the community over the years. Topics of possible interest for such an oral history might be the origins of the industry in the area, its early impact on the local economy, labor-management relationships and their changes across time, a typical working day in 1930 as opposed to now, changes in general working conditions, problems of worker safety and environmental pollution, and significant incidents in the history of the local industry (strikes, layoffs, disasters, boom periods, etc.).

An Immigrants Oral History
To begin with, it is well to remember that all Americans are immigrants. The fact that some immigrated earlier than others should not cast any aspersions on the latecomers! The many persons in the community who either came to this country in their lifetimes or who

were told about that coming by their parents offer a fascinating subject for the classroom oral history project. In many cases only oral history can document their experiences before they are forgotten.[17]

The project could focus on the experiences of community members of a single national origin or of several such groups. The immigrants project could seek to answer such questions as: What do the immigrants remember about their original homeland? Why did they (or their parents) decide to come to this country? How did they come over, and at what port of entry did they arrive? What do they remember about the checking in process? Where did they or their family first take up residence? What were the most difficult problems of cultural adjustment to the family's new circumstances? How strong are present ties to the old language, culture, and nation of origin? In planning the immigrants oral history project students might wish to study the most recent groups of immigrants to the community and how they are adapting to their new life (for example, Vietnamese, Cubans, and Mexicans).

Environmental Oral History

Students interview elderly persons about their personal experience of changes in the local environment during their lifetimes, and the oral traditions about that environment passed down from informants' parents and grandparents. For example: Are there oral traditions (or written records) about what the community site was like at the time of the first settlement? What impressed early settlers about the locality? How have the landscape, flora, and fauna changed from the time of the first settlement? How have they changed from the late nineteenth century? What was the area like at the turn of the century? In the 1920s? What have been the major changes in local land use over the last half century? Why did these shifts in human-land relationship come about? What are the present trends? If the community is in an urban area, what has been the evolution of its urban environment?

A Trades and Professions Project

For many persons in the community, the most vivid part of their life experience will relate to their work—their trade or profession. This oral history project would focus upon that work experience and record and analyze changes in community trades and professions across the decades. Potential informants for the trades and professions project include (among many others) former carpenters, cigar makers, doctors, lawyers, plumbers, housewives, nurses, milliners, and blacksmiths. The project might choose to concentrate on the study of a single trade or profession of particular importance to the home community, or it might decide to sample as many as possible. The individual interview in the trades and professions project would be a variety of the topical life history, focusing on the individual's work experience. It would explore the reasons why the subjects entered their specialty, changes in the specialty they have observed over time, etc.

The Local Effects of National Events: Hypotheses Testing
In the hypotheses testing project, students use oral history to test the local effects of significant historical developments in national and international life. Suitable topics for this type of oral history study are any of those covered in the U.S. history textbook occurring within the lifetimes of living residents in the community, for example, the World Wars, the "roaring twenties," the Depression, the civil rights movement, Vietnam and the peace movement, etc.

As in the case of the study of the Great Depression discussed earlier (see the case studies section), the basic pattern is as follows: (1) Students and teacher choose a suitable topic from the textbook. (2) Beginning with the text, and then going to secondary and primary sources about the target event, students devise a series of tentative hypotheses about how they believe the event would have affected the home community. (3) These tentative hypotheses are converted into a series of research questions with which to approach local informants. The questions are designed to elicit oral history testimony to either support or reject the tentative hypotheses. (4) Oral history interviews are conducted with a carefully selected group of community informants. (5) Finally, based on these interviews, tentative conclusions are reached about the hypotheses.

The Oral History of a Significant Local Event
Students use oral history to study some event in the community past that community persons believe to be especially significant. This would be a purely local event, something which may have raised not a ripple on the state or national scene, but which has been defined as important by the local community itself. Such an event could be a flood, fire, tornado, or other natural disaster. It could be a local scandal, a murder and/or sensational murder trial, or the coming of a major new industry to the area. The common denominators of such

events are that the event is almost entirely local in its effects and that community persons are united in their belief that the event is of considerable significance for the local past.

All communities have such benchmark events in their traditional histories (for some reason, many of them seem to be disasters), and preliminary questioning of several older residents will probably reveal a number of candidates. Once students have agreed on the local event they plan to study and have collected some information about it, they should draw up an interview guide and begin to conduct systematic interviews with local folks about what really happened.

At this point, if the class has chosen the right event, things will begin to get very interesting! Teachers and students should be advised that to the extent the target event is truly important to community tradition, there will be competing views of the event in community oral tradition, and these differing versions will be adhered to with a certain amount of heat and vehemence. (Be warned; the mere fact that local people choose to remember a particular event suggests that it is still at some level a "live issue" for the community.)

The oral history data about the target event lend themselves to two rather different kinds of historical analysis, and the project might explore both possibilities. In the main aspect of the study, the class should sift through the conflicting testimony to arrive at a tentative conclusion about what really happened and why. This judgment would be reached on the basis of internal and external evidence in the community testimony and the supporting evidence from documentary sources. In the second part of the study, the class might examine the full range of community opinion about the event as a study in folk history—something true in belief if not in fact. Questions to raise at this point are: Why do people choose to remember the event in the way they do? Is there evidence that elements of pure folklore have drifted in to elaborate upon the kernels of historical truth? Are the different ways in which people remember the event related to the structure of community relationships at the time the event occurred? Are they related to community social structure in the present?

Chronicling Recent Local Events with Oral History
Although superficially similar to the previous idea, this project option is really very different. The subject of this study is an important *recent* event in community history—something that happened within the last few months. Students will find themselves retracing the steps of local news reporters a few days, weeks, or months after the event.

Their purpose is to interview participants and eyewitnesses to combine the approaches of oral history and investigative journalism for a
description of what really happened—an account that may or may
not be in substantial agreement with what the local news media originally reported. Students may discover conflicting testimony neglected by local reporters, eyewitnesses who have changed their
stories since they were interviewed by the press, and many other
instructive phenomena. This kind of oral history project can give students a sense of what it is like to work with historical data when they
are still "warm."

Institutional or Organizational Histories
As a class project, students research and write an oral history of a
significant local institution or organization. Churches, local businesses, clubs, schools, fraternal or professional organizations—all
provide suitable objects of study for the institutional oral history
project. There are several advantages to this kind of project. The institution chosen for study is usually clearly defined in time and
space, and often has kept good enough records to provide a documentary backbone for the research. Institutional members are usually more than willing to contribute to the study, ready to come to
the school to be interviewed, and to help in other ways. After deciding on an appropriate institution or organization to research, students formulate appropriate questions and interview knowledgeable
persons to prepare its formal history.

An Oral History of Traditional Crafts
In the retentive minds and skilled hands of certain persons in the
community, the past still lingers into the present. These are the persons knowledgeable about certain traditional crafts and skills once
widely practiced in the area but now almost forgotten. Some of these
traditional craftspersons may still be practicing their archaic skill;
others may not have done so for decades, retaining only the memory
of how to do it. Both kinds of informants are excellent subjects for an
oral history of traditional crafts.

  Traditional crafts are folk crafts in the sense that they are usually
learned informally and taught by word of mouth and demonstration
from earlier craftspersons. Many of these crafts are direct inheri-
tances from the nineteenth century, when households and communities had to produce many more of the objects of daily life. The
various *Foxfire* anthologies are a matchless compendium of these
traditional crafts, as well as excellent examples of the sort of student

oral history project described here. *Foxfire's* students have located and interviewed community persons who showed them how to rive shingles, construct log houses, whittle, make folk toys, construct sunbonnets, build brush brooms, churn milk to make butter, make a basket out of white oak splints, sew a quilt, preserve vegetables and fruits, make lye soap, use herbal remedies, shuck corn, plow with a mule, weave on a loom, tan hides, make dipper gourds, make cornshuck mops/dolls/hats, identify wild plant foods, build a dry stone wall, make bird traps/deadfalls/rabbit boxes, make folk instruments, construct a homemade water jug, do simple blacksmithing, and wash clothes in an iron pot.

What else? Find out from folks in your community what *they* know. And do not make the assumption that your community is too urban—too "uptown"—to have traditional crafts and craftspersons; it almost certainly is not! Steps in the oral history of traditional crafts are: (1) locate a community person who knows how to do some old folk craft or skill and will demonstrate it for you; (2) take a student research team out to tape-record and photograph the process as the person demonstrates and describes it; (3) using the craftsperson's own words and your photos of the various stages of the process, put together an oral history/photojournalism essay on how to do it. This essay should be sufficiently clear and detailed so that others could successfully perform the traditional craft from your description. Again, the *Foxfire* books provide excellent illustrations of the end products of this kind of classroom oral history.

Studies in Community Social History
Someone once observed that social history was that 95 percent of human experience in the past that was left over after historians had finished writing their official histories—their "History with a capital H." What is certain is that the many common elements of everyday life in the past lend themselves to study by way of oral history. Here are a few of the many possible topics about life in the home community some fifty years ago that might become the subject of classroom study: home heating and cooling, roads and transportation systems (trolleys, streetcars), celebrations and how to celebrate them, sports and other community recreations, courtship and marriage practices, standards of community morality—the list is all but endless. And keep in mind that anyone who lived in the community fifty years ago will have direct personal experience of most of these aspects of everyday life in the past. For an oral history of community social life, everyone is a bona fide expert.

Social History: Then and Now Studies
As a variation of the social history project, students use oral history to collect information about how the topic in community social life was handled then (fifty years ago) as opposed to the way it is handled now.

This is possible because problems in community social life are perennial and persistent, as ubiquitous as the proverbial "death and taxes" (which, incidentally, are perfectly good research topics). In the then and now project, students use their knowledge about present-day practices as a point of departure for oral history fieldwork into the way things were done in the past. Students explore the past dimensions of their research topics by interviewing their own grandparents and/or other adults of their grandparents' generation. For example, students might begin by asking themselves about the contemporary pattern of courtship and marriage, or food preservation, or some other detail of day-to-day life. As they gather information about the past dimension of their research topic, they keep careful notes about their informants' testimony. Then they write an essay of comparison and contrast, comparing the way things were done circa 1930 with the way the same things are done today.

Again, as in the general project in social history, a wide range of topics is possible. To the greatest extent practicable, individual students should be free to choose and explore subjects of personal interest to them.

Social History: Ethnic Variations
Just as elements of social life vary across time, so they vary across ethnic group boundaries—across culture. If several ethnicities are represented in the classroom and community, the class may opt for a variant of the social history study in which students use oral history to compare and contrast the way in which different ethnic groups deal with similar aspects of social life. What are, for example, the similarities and the differences between black, Anglo, and Mexican-American child-rearing practices (or courtship, or folk medicine) of a half-century ago? It might be interesting to find out. The class could choose a limited range of topics to explore, use oral history interviews to collect cross-ethnic data on each topic, and then compare and contrast the different approaches to solving the perennial problems of social life. The idea is to use oral history as a practical exercise in cultural pluralism. Here, as elsewhere, the intent is to approach cultural differences as an enrichment and a resource for the community, something to celebrate rather than something to ignore

or gloss over. Any of the many potential topics in community life may be explored in its ethnic variation by use of oral history. Remember, in a multiethnic community local history is also ethnic studies.

Ethnic History Projects

As discussed in chapter 1, oral history is a powerful strategy for creating the raw materials of a community ethnic history from scratch when few documentary sources exist. Over a semester or a school year, students can collect oral history interviews for a general history of their ethnic group in the community from earliest times to the present.[18] Such a history is likely to be a combination of traditional chronological narrative and social history. The basic purpose of such projects is to discover, document, and celebrate the contributions to community life made by each ethnicity. Does your school have an especially diverse ethnic makeup? Perhaps each semester all students in a given class might work on the community history of a single ethnic group. Both the explorations of one's own ethnic roots and the study of another person's have their benefits.

The Study of a Local Campaign or Election

The field research methodology of oral history is applicable to community-study projects outside the area of traditional history, for example, to the study of local government. Just as community history is the most accessible history for study by way of the classroom oral history project, so are the forms and processes of community political life most accessible to field study by the political science class.

In one project possibility, students might combine interviewing and participant observation in the study of a local election campaign in progress. Certain students, acting in terms of their own political convictions and preferences, might work on a campaign staff or staffs, while others interview campaign participants. Students who collected material in the field could be debriefed in class on a weekly basis. Data collected by way of observation and interview could be used as basic data for a class analysis of the campaign.

Alternatively, students might use oral history interviews to study some momentous campaign in the recent or not so recent past: Reagan versus Carter, for example, or Carter versus Ford. They could also study legendary local electoral battles in county or community politics—colorful campaigns about which local politicos are fond of reminiscing. (As they embark on these or other projects in their local political study, students and teacher might take heed of the words of T. Harry Williams in the introduction to his prize-winning biography of the "Kingfish," Huey P. Long of Louisiana: "As I continued with the research, I became increasingly convinced of the validity of oral history. Not only was it a necessary tool in compiling the history of the recent past, but it also provided an unusually intimate look into that past. I found that the politicians were astonishingly frank in detailing their motives, and often completely realistic in viewing themselves. But they had not trusted a record of these dealings to paper, and it would not have occurred to them to transcribe their experiences at a later time. Anybody who heard them would have to conclude that the full and inside story of politics is not in *any* age committed to the documents.")[19]

Political Studies: A Controversy Retrospective
Students might interview a variety of persons on different sides of present-day community political controversies and conduct a historical "retrospective" on the origins and development of these live issues by way of oral history. All communities have such issues: the placement of a local park, zoning changes, busing and school integration, and the like. In this application of oral history, the political science class explores the historical roots of the controversy, not with the presumption of resolving it, but with the intent to integrate these conflicting and often emotional testimonies to arrive at some balanced view of the issue.

Political Studies: Local Lives in Politics
Students in the government class might do topical life histories of the active (or retired) participants in local political life, including both incumbents and those persons presently on the "outside." The topic of these life histories is the individual's life in politics. Once again, the model for this kind of study might be T. Harry Williams's biography of Huey P. Long. Students are likely to find that local politicians make very good interview subjects, and that their lives offer fascinating insights into both the political process and the reason for their personal involvement in it.

Political Studies: Local Political Roles
In a related but different study, students might focus not upon the person, but the person's conception of the office. Students might interview present and past political officeholders to gather data about how they view their office, its purposes, powers, limitations, responsibilities, and problems. Such a study could focus upon role variation (e.g., the different ways present county commissioners view their

role) or on role change (e.g., the difference between the way in which a sheriff of the 1930s and the current sheriff see their offices). Students are likely to find that this latter alternative, the study of changes in office holders' role conceptions across time, will be a particularly interesting application of oral history to the study of local government. Such studies may be done of past and present city and county officials of all kinds. In fact, in small town and rural environments the sheriff is often an excellent candidate.

Political Studies: The Structure of Local Politics
In a research project concerned with determining the principal actors (past and present) in the local political scene, students might conduct interviews designed to map a rough outline of the people and groups actively and recurrently involved in local political life. This study could focus on the formal outline, the political parties and other formal political organizations, and/or could delve into informal and de facto political groups—cliques, lobbies, etc. By way of oral history interviews, students might trace the way in which the current political structure has evolved and changed over the last half century.

Political Studies: Local Political Meetings
Here students might analyze the process and substance of local political decision making as revealed in political meetings that are open to the public (city council meetings, meetings of the county commissioners, etc.). The meetings could be field-recorded for debriefing in class. Of course, such public meetings are but the tip of the iceberg of the local political process. Students should listen to the transcripts and ask the collective question, "What's really going on here?" The often enigmatic surface of events at such a meeting should be taken as a point of departure for a research study, using oral history interviews to determine some reasonable answers to that question. Students might interview meeting participants, local political observers, newspaper reporters, and others about the recent history of local politics with regard to topics covered in the meetings.

Political Studies: Political Folklore
Politics, the art and craft of making policy decisions, generates its own forms of folklore, and students can go out into the community (and especially among politicians) to collect it. Be assured, local Republicans can be persuaded to tell Democrat jokes and vice versa. In addition, students may discover versions of what folklorist Allen Dun-

des calls "folklore from the paperwork empire"—humorous graphic
references on the political process processed and duplicated by the
ubiquitous Xerox machine. Some of this political folklore will have
reference to current political figures, and some may have considerable time depth. Don't neglect to ask about political slogans, campaign songs, and the like. Political folklore offers a fascinating (if
irreverent) glimpse into the real world of local politics.

Folklore Studies: A Self-Interview
In a folkloric counterpart to the very first project idea in this section
(the oral autobiography), students treat themselves as their own informant and collect all the folklore that they themselves know.

The line between oral history and folklore in living oral tradition
is often difficult to determine; there is, in fact, a considerable degree
of overlap and interpenetration between the two. Strictly speaking,
folklore is the verbal folk art of the social group, which is transmitted
orally, person-to-person, and is not usually written down. It varies
from ethnic group to ethnic group, from region to region, and from
generation to generation (students, for example, have their own folklore). In an enterprise closely linked to the study of community social
history, students in social studies or English classes might locate, record, transcribe, and analyze a variety of folklore from the community, ethnic groups, families, peers, and from themselves.

In this introductory project, students begin by treating themselves as the informants and collecting all the folklore they know—
jokes, riddles, and the like. Some general categories of folklore are
folk sayings, riddles, proverbs, "tom swifties," cruelty jokes, ethnic or
"aggie" jokes, legend and belief tales, ghost stories, folk remedies,
jump-rope rhymes, weather signs, graffiti, "luck" superstitions, animal
lore, songs, and tall tales. (The first thing for the folklore project to do
is to obtain some general work that includes a typology of the different genres [kinds] of folklore. For this purpose, we especially recommend the works of Richard and Laura Tallman, Elaine S. Katz, Jan
Brunvaud, and Barre Toelken.)[20] Here, in this introductory project,
students use tape recorder or notepad to systematically work
through a list of folklore types and record all the folklore that they
personally know and use.

Folklore Studies: Student Folklore
Although folklore like anything else can be approached historically,
folklore is not just "old stuff"; living folklore is at least halfway believed in. A case in point is the so-called "urban legend" or "belief

tale," which is usually told as true. Students are certain to know a long series of these, including (perhaps) the story about the "death car," the lady with the beehive hairdo (which she never combed out and which came to shelter vermin), the devil's appearance in a local bar or disco, or "the veterinarian's revenge." Various "ghost" or "moving light" stories that students tell are of this ilk, but please remember that these kinds of stories are often told as true and are at least partially believed in. This quasibelief is what gives them their cutting edge!

In the student folklore project class members collect belief tales and any of a wide range of other folklore types from their fellow students on the school premises. The class project could focus on one genre of folklore at a time, or give students free rein to collect multiple forms. In folklorists' terms, collection could be either in a natural or an artificial context. In a natural context approach, students would not ask for elements of folklore but simply listen for them to occur in normal social interaction among their peers. An artificial context approach would explicitly elicit folklore. A student might say, "Do you know the one about . . ." or "Do you know any more 'tom swifties'?"

Folklore Studies: Children's Folklore

Students may be initially surprised to find out that children have their own forms of folklore that are passed down from child to child across the generations of childhood. However, a little introspection will allow students to begin to delve these up from their own childhood memories. After a refresher course in children's folklore, the class might embark on a project to collect a wide range of such materials from younger brothers and sisters and other neighborhood children. As they do so, students might pay careful attention to the way in which children use their folklore, i.e., its social and psychological function in the play group.[21]

Children's folklore takes many forms and, while such folklore is always changing, some of the variants of children's folklore are quite old. The following verse, for example, has been collected in nearly identical texts in widely separated parts of the United States and in England:

> Quick, quick
> The cat's been sick.
> Where? Where?
> Under the chair.
> Hasten, hasten,

Fetch the basin.
Kate, Kate,
You're far too late,
The rug is in a dreadful state!

Children's folklore includes jump-rope rhymes, ball-bouncing rhymes, counting-out rhymes, nonsense rhymes, autograph album rhymes, taunts, riddle jokes (Question: "What has four wheels and flies?" Answer: "A garbage truck"), and a wide variety of verbal materials in association with games such as kickball, tag and chase, kissing games, guessing games, ring or circle games, team games, and the like. Students in the project could collect these materials in natural context as they observe children after school or at school recess. Alternatively, they could interview children about what they know.

Folklore Studies: Family Folklore
In a family folklore project, using some kind of checklist of the various kinds of folklore, students might interview their immediate family members to collect what they know. The search could be for a few varieties of folklore or for a very large number, but the family project probably would be most interesting if students would try for a comprehensive collection of family lore. Here, as elsewhere, they might note the way in which historical elements and folkloric elements intermingle in memory and oral testimony.[22] This intermingling of historic "truth" and folkloric "falsehood" is a natural process; for example, consider the case of the local mass murder (fact) and its association with stories about a haunted house in the community (fiction, presumably!). Students should accumulate their family folklore collections over a period of days using tape recorder or notepad, and then bring their family folklore anthology to class for comparison with others.

Folklore Studies: A Community-Wide Collection
As a class project, students collect a single folklore genre (the ghost story, the riddle, etc.) from a large number of persons in the community. Such a project would begin with those variants of the target folklore that students and their families know, but would go on to become a comprehensive survey of the community. Students might interview persons who live in their home neighborhoods, family friends, and others, and could collect additional forms of the target folklore by way of the telephone. The result of the research could be a comprehensive anthology of a single form, or limited range of

forms, of community folklore. The pattern could be repeated later for another genre of folklore.

Folklore Studies: Ethnic Variations in Folklore
As in the case of social history, different ethnicities in the community mean increased possibilities. Students are likely to find that different ethnic groups have somewhat different classes of folklore, tell different forms within those classes, and use folklore in different ways in their social interactions. All of this ethnic variation makes a fertile subject for field research in folklore. Students in the class might collect folklore within their ethnicity or across ethnic lines (there are advantages to both options), and they might bring these collections to class for purposes of comparison and contrast. Again, as in the study of social history, the ethnic folklore project is a practical celebration of community cultural diversity.

3 / Technical Matters

While the choice of topics is certainly important, the basics of how to go about doing oral history—the real nuts and bolts—require careful attention. Before turning our attention to the interview itself, let's explore some of the technical aspects of the interview process.

Tape Recorders

For years, oral history depended on the memory of the interviewer or on rough notes taken during the interview. The introduction of the wire recorder, and ultimately the tape recorder, changed oral history procedures dramatically. Today almost all oral history projects employ tape recorders to collect interview data.

Tape recorders are classified in one of two ways, depending on the tape format used. Reel-to-reel tape recorders are used for such purposes as the recording and presentation of music because of the quality of sound reproduction. Other tape recorders use cassette tapes, which are already packaged in plastic containers and require no threading.

Professional oral history programs that are well funded, such as the one at Columbia University, always use reel-to-reel recorders because of the quality of the recording. An additional reason for using reel-to-reel tape recorders (and probably the strongest argument for their use) is the significant preservation advantages they offer. A high quality reel-to-reel tape under ideal conditions of temperature and humidity may reasonably be expected to last one hundred and twenty-five years or more. A cassette tape of equal quality may not last even twenty-five years.

While a great many oral historians would argue for a reel-to-reel format, almost every oral history project in public schools uses cassette recorders. The reasons for doing so are probably obvious. Students are more familiar with and have an easier time operating a cassette tape recorder. Cassette recorders are easier to carry to an interview. Cassette tapes take up less space in storage.

Indeed, we would recommend cassette tape recorders as the easiest, most inexpensive route for you to take. Why spend the money and encourage the inconvenience of a large, expensive, and undoubtedly fragile machine for use by students, when a small, portable machine will do? Having said that, however, in the same breath we would encourage you to buy the highest quality cassette machine you can afford. An inexpensive machine may not be cost effective, particularly when the transcription process involves so much starting and stopping. An inexpensive machine will quickly retire itself, adding to your capital outlays and, in some cases, delaying the interview process.

Several features are of inestimable value when considering which machine to buy. Does your contemplated machine have battery and AC adapter options? Most of the time, an AC adapter is preferable to batteries, because batteries are expensive and often unreliable. Yet occasionally your students will be away from an electrical outlet and will need the flexibility that batteries provide.

While on the subject of batteries, most advisers we talked to suggested using the relatively recent alkaline batteries rather than the old carbon-zinc variety. The alkaline batteries last longer and seem to have a better shelf life. A few projects have gone to the rechargeable batteries, but most consider the initial cost of rechargeables to be more than they want to spend.

Batteries, when used, should always be tested first. Some machines will continue to operate on low power, producing a distorted, "chipmunk" voice that is almost impossible to transcribe. Even those projects that use batteries switch to an AC adapter for playback and transcription, because the constant rewinding and fast forwarding required for transcription is very energy consuming. Batteries, if used at all, should only be employed for recording the interview. Even fast forwarding and rewinding during the interview should be done while the recorder is plugged into an electrical outlet in order to avoid rapid depletion of the batteries.

An excellent feature on some tape recorders is the VU meter, which indicates by means of a needle the sound level of the recording being made. With a VU meter a student can monitor the sound level of a recording in progress. A quick glance at the VU needle permits a student to ascertain immediately if a recorder is functioning. The VU meter usually has an area to the extreme right marked in red, indicating that the voice level (or gain) is too high. The desired position is about midway, with only occasional peaks in the red.

Another handy device on most tape recorders is a counter, which can be manually set to zero. The counter can be used to locate information on the tape. However, counters will not count the same in different models of tape recorders, and even in different machines of the same model. Additionally, many operators forget to set the counter to zero when beginning an interview (or a tape side), making the use of the counter even more problematic. Yet when remembered, they can be used as a rapid (if gross) locating device.

One of the keys to successful recording is an adequate microphone. Most of the inexpensive recorders have built-in condenser microphones. While these do pick up human voices, they are also notorious for recording machine noises, or low hums. The best recordings are made with external microphones, *placed as close as possible to the speakers*. One ideal microphone system, used in one university oral history project, was a dual lavaliere microphone system, with one microphone clipped on the collar or lapel of the interviewer, the other on the collar or lapel of the interviewee. When the microphones are as close as possible to each other, background noise is often completely eliminated. The problem with such a system is that interviewer and interviewee are inseparably linked by wires. Even if a lavaliere system is not available or desired, an external microphone is virtually a necessity. An on-off switch on the microphone will allow the interviewer to pause without the cumbersome button pushing required to stop a machine that may be placed some distance away.

Recording Tape
On the matter of what kind of tape to use, most oral history projects are unanimous. Buy the best you can afford! If you are using cassette tapes, this means purchasing only C-60 tapes (30 minutes per side). The reason for this is simple: C-60 tapes use 1.5 mil (thickness) tape. Anything thinner has two significant disadvantages. First, thinner tapes have a tendency to break, ruining an interview and wasting time. Second, thinner tapes have a tendency to "bleed through," allowing the recording on one part of the tape to be transferred to another part of the tape it is touching in the cassette, particularly after long storage.

Tape storage can be facilitated by purchasing tape storage containers, commercially available from library supply houses. Your school librarian probably has a catalog from one or more of these companies (Gaylord Company, for example). Tape storage boxes permit the orderly preservation of your collected material.

Recording Procedures
If there is one standard in the field of oral history, it is "know your equipment!" More grief has been caused by a lack of understanding of recording equipment than can be imagined. The tape recorder should be an unobtrusive part of an interview, a quiet machine that sits on the periphery of an intensive interaction between two people. When the interviewer does not know the equipment, the interview often focuses on the problems of the tape recorder rather than on the narrative of the interviewee.

The only way to insure familiarity is to make students use tape recorders in noninterview situations until they are familiar with them. Often trial interviews are done by students using other students as interviewees. This gives students practice in the many dimensions of interviewing, which helps ensure that the actual experience is more professional.

One preliminary way for students to familiarize themselves with the capacities of their particular recorder is for them to play what Edward Ives calls the "game." If your machine has a VU meter, position your tape recorder so that you can see the meter from some distance away. Then put a tape in, set the machine on record mode, and begin to talk, all the time telling yourself what you are doing and how the machine is responding at the moment. Ives offers this hypothetical example of the process:

> Now I've turned the thing on, and I'm talking in my normal voice directly in front of the mike and about two feet from it. . . . The needle on the VU meter is moving up to but not into the red area. Now I'm moving back to about four feet from the mike and I haven't changed anything else, and the needle is only moving up about a quarter of the way, except when I SHOUT, when it jumps up almost to the red. OK, now I'm moving over to the right to about forty-five degrees, still about four feet away, and the needle is hardly moving at all, just a little. Now I'm moving in to turn the machine some so I can see the meter from over here—I haven't moved the mike or changed anything else—and OK now I'm back out again at four feet, and the needle isn't moving at all now. Now I'm directly behind the mike, and the needle still isn't moving, even when I SHOUT—well, it did move just a little then, but . . .[1]

Ives recommends that you keep this game up for some time, trying different settings, distances, and noise levels and always telling yourself where you are relative to the machine and what the VU meter is doing at the time. If the machine has a built-in microphone, try that, and then immediately after try the external microphone. Try turning on an electric fan or TV in the background. If you have a cardioid microphone, what happens when you aim it straight up? Take your time and try everything, all the time telling yourself and the machine what you are doing. Ives's exercise is an efficient way to learn about the particular capacities (and idiosyncracies) of your tape recorder. Once you play the game, you really know what your machine can and cannot do.

During an actual interview, many interviewers begin by testing their machines in the presence of the interviewee. A short piece of conversation, an introduction to the tape, or even a description of the weather can serve as a short opening test sample that guarantees that the recording equipment is functioning adequately.

One of the most difficult problems in interview recording is background noise. Some microphones have automatic level control, which means that they react automatically to variations in sound level. While this is sometimes helpful, often the automatic level control tends to reduce voice level in favor of some other louder noise in the room. One of the difficulties with background noise is gauging its impact on the recorder. For example, you are visiting with someone in a living room, while dishes are being washed in the kitchen. The noise of the dishwashing doesn't disturb the interview but later, replaying the tape, the sound of dishes being washed is all that can be heard. One author recalls an important interview he once conducted some eighteen hundred miles from home. The interview took place in the study of the interviewee's home. Unbeknown to the interviewer, the chair in which he was sitting had a loud squeak, which occurred each time he shifted his weight. While the squeak was hardly noticed during the interview, it was almost the only noise that could be heard in the tape recording, dominating all other noises.

The ideal for your students is simple. Make certain that they are well versed in the operation of their tape recorder. Have them test the recorder at the beginning of each interview. Finally, suggest that during some break in the interview, interviewers listen to a brief portion to insure that the recording being made is a good one.

Preliminary Planning

Crucial to any successful oral history project is careful and adequate preparation in topic selection, background research, and development of an interview guide. Each of these important components must be done by you *and* by your students.

Selection of Topic(s)

One of the basic tenets of this new approach to learning is that students must be involved in their own education. That involvement must occur at the very outset, as you first begin to plan for your project. As chapter 2 indicates, the number of possible topics is mind-boggling. Only you and your students can select topics that are appropriate to your local area, grade level, and ability. A key decision involves selection of topics. What are your students interested in? One project investigated the history of a local leash law for pets and community sentiment about that law. That seems like a simplistic idea. Yet the overriding fact is that students were interested in it, they got involved in studying because of it, and they learned research and writing skills from it.

What topics might you and your students select? What kinds of unique histories (people, places, things) lie close by? What items could be easily researched? What kinds of topics might have written, as well as oral, sources for comparison and contrast? What topics can your students handle effectively? These are important questions that must be answered early.

Background Information

Once you have selected a topic, plan on doing some background research. Assume you've selected "Experiences during the Great Depression in Yourville" as your topic. Obviously your students must learn a great deal about the Depression in order to ask intelligent questions. What was the government's role in the 1930s, for example? What is a depression? What were some typical experiences throughout America during this period? You may want to show a film, assign readings, give classroom lectures. In short, you will want to *teach* something about the Depression in order to give students a context within which they may *learn* about the Depression.

One method for preparing students for interviewing is the creation of hypotheses, mentioned in chapter 2. The goal of hypothesis formation is to structure students for historical inquiry. For example, you may wish to examine "Experiences in Wartime" as a topic. You may hypothesize that World War II and Vietnam were very different kinds of wars for their participants. That hypothesis could then be tested by interviewing individuals who had seen service in those wars.

Interview Guide

The final preparation that you must consider includes the creation of an interview guide, a list of suggested topics or areas that would logically be covered in a thorough interview. Again, these must be derived by students and teacher together. Very little understanding will be achieved if students are given a guide without having contributed to its creation.

The interview guide should be distinguished from instructions given interviewers that are largely procedural in nature. For example, you will probably want to prepare a checklist for interviewers that will include these items: Has the legal release form been signed? Is the interviewer data sheet filled out? Was the tape begun with an introduction? Were photographs taken? These procedural matters are very important to ensure some consistency in the way students go about interviewing.

An interview guide, on the other hand, suggests questions and topics for that particular interview. An interview about the great flood of 1947, for example, might include some preliminary questions about the background of the interviewee, then move to the specific location of the individual at the time of the flood, and finally focus on specific recollections of the flood. The guide might remind interviewers to ask about relatives or friends lost in the flood or personal feelings during its occurrence. The development of the guide is a helpful way to teach students that sometimes questions asked a certain way will produce certain responses. The discussion of the guide will also be an excellent time to remind students to ask open-ended questions, which allow for a variety of responses. In the formulation of the guide, students may even learn that the best interviewers often ask the same question two or three different ways in order to evoke the richest response.

Having created the interview guide, however, be warned that some students will try to use it as a mechanical checklist. Nothing could be further from its intended use. The interview guide is just that, a guide. It should direct and focus the interview in some preplanned ways; under no circumstances should it control the interview. The interview is a difficult situation, as we will discuss later, that requires skill, tact, and mental adroitness to successfully complete. Despite the guide, interviews should go where they will, tapping unexpected memories and opening new inquiries. The guide can be a very handy device for finding these hidden memories. Used mechanically, however, it can stifle the most loquacious interviewee.

In the Field
Interview Situations

We wish to note here some of the mechanical dimensions of the interview situation. The ideal interview is conducted in a home or other relaxed setting, where the interviewee feels comfortable. Interviews can last an hour to two hours at one sitting; most people have a difficult time being interviewed for a longer stretch. The interview setting should be quiet, with no fans, television, or radio on. An inside room is preferable to a porch or outside area.

The interviewee should be at ease for the interview. Some interviewers, acutely aware of the uneasiness of the situation, work too hard to make the interviewee feel comfortable before starting. They leaf through photo albums or engage in an extended discussion, hoping to establish rapport with the subject. Unfortunately, the result is usually not what was hoped for; reminiscences are lost because the tape recorder wasn't on or time is wasted that could have been used productively.

The tape recorder should be within easy reach of the interviewer but not between the interviewer and the interviewee. Having the tape recorder as a prominent and visible reminder of the recording process sometimes intimidates the speaker. One interviewer recommended putting the tape recorder on the floor, near the chair of the interviewer but out of direct sight of the interviewee. Only the microphone then was placed between speaker and listener.

The position of the microphone is critical to the success of the interview. If you do not have a dual microphone arrangement (described earlier in the chapter), the microphone must be placed between the two interview participants. If the voice of the interviewer is fairly strong, the microphone can be tilted toward the interviewee.

The surface the microphone is placed on is also important. A table, for example, may cause some distortion in voices as sound waves bounce off the hard surface. If the microphone moves, the noise of course is magnified on the recording. One simple means for ensuring better recordings is to carry along a cloth (about the size of a wash cloth) on which to rest the microphone. This softens the voices and prevents any background noise from being recorded if the microphone moves or is jiggled.

Many oral history projects send two people out to interview, some even more than that. We would recommend two but suspect that any more would cause more problems than they would solve. The second person serves as moral support, the importance of which, with students, should not be discounted. There are also technical matters that a second person can resolve without interrupting the interview. For example, the second person can set up and monitor the recording equipment, keep the room quiet, check to see that forms are properly filled out, and even take photographs. A second person can also make mental note of omissions, discrepancies, questions, and other substantive matters that the principal interviewer, intent on listening, may fail to notice.

Photography and Photographs
Almost every oral history project uses photographs, both of informants and those that embellish and enliven the substance of the interview itself. As color photography is expensive to process and reproduce in journals, most student projects use black and white film. A good single lens reflex 35 mm camera is typically used, because it allows for a great deal of versatility. If you do not have funds for the purchase of your own camera, the school may have one you can borrow. Some schools send a school photographer to act as second interviewer, taking care of technical details and photographing the interview as well.

Old photographs can be an invaluable source of information and interest, enriching the recollections with the vivid impression of being there. Invariably, informants have old photos that they may be willing to share long enough to be copied. Copying black and white photographs is a relatively simple and inexpensive process, particularly if your school has a photographic darkroom.

Field Notes
Students should be encouraged to take notes in the field for a variety of reasons. Some notes will be reminders to check on something when back in the project office. Other notes are made during the interview to ask about something that was mentioned but that would interrupt the train of thought if pursued immediately. For example, an interviewee might mention a diary during a long discussion of his battle experiences in World War I. That diary would be invaluable. Yet to interrupt the discussion of this particular battle might destroy the segment, when a later reference to that diary would have done

just as well. In interviewing, interruptions should be kept to a minimum. Questions of clarification, derived from notes, can be as illuminating as interruptions without the attendant risks.

Forms
Inevitably, forms are required in a project to record information and protect individual rights.

Interview Data Sheet
Most oral history projects use a form to record biographical information about the interviewee, as well as data about the interview itself. The biographical information, depending on the nature of the project, usually includes the interviewee's place and date of birth, names of family members, work experiences, and the like. The interview data include such things as date and location of the interview, name of interviewer(s), number of tapes, and special remarks (see appendix II).

Legal Release
The legal release clarifies the conditions under which an oral interview is made. It acknowledges the legal (and legitimate) rights of interviewees to shield themselves from public ridicule or the betrayal of confidences. Generally, legal releases either give complete access to an interview or stipulate the conditions under which all or portions of the interview will be released. The memoirs of politicians and other well-known public figures are often closed for a stipulated number of years or until the death of the memoirist. Rarely, an interview is even sealed for a number of years after death, to protect reputations or avoid legal battles.

Most student oral history projects have no difficulty with the legal release form; that is, most people are willing to sign the release without questions. Occasionally, interviewees ask to see the transcript of their interview, prior to release, or ask that any published material be approved by them prior to publication. Your own instincts and experience will guide you best in this matter. A great deal depends on the nature of the people you interview and the reputation of your project.

What you must protect against is possible legal liability. The only way to avoid litigation is to have an approved legal release form and make certain that it is signed by all parties prior to publication. "All parties" means interviewee *and* interviewer, because some court cases have suggested that both the informant and the person asking questions have legal rights to any verbatim transcript and that both are considered authors. Even if you do win a lawsuit, you have in effect lost, for the cost of the attorney and any resulting notoriety will have damaged your project, possibly fatally.

A sample release form is found in appendix I. However, your school attorney (or one on your board, or a parent) should probably examine yours to verify that it meets requirements of both state and federal laws.

While legal releases are generally signed without comment, there may be instances of refusal. There have even been one or two lawsuits over the unapproved publication of material from oral history interviews, although the interview was made by students and not some publisher interested in profits. The greatest problem remains the *threat* of lawsuit. You, as project adviser, must simply emphasize the need to get that legal release signed. Some projects have releases signed during the first interview, some later in the process, and some only ask for releases at the time of publication. Obviously, the longer you wait, the greater the chance that the interviewee may die. On the other hand, getting a signature at the first interview may arouse some suspicions. Pam Wood, of the *Salt* project, notes some of the problems she has had with release forms.

> Some of us have been put in the awkward position of re-membering that the release forms weren't signed *after* a story has gone to the printer and have had to do some scrambling to get them signed. We have had no one refuse to sign a form, but we make it a practice not to ask for signatures on the first interview. Our people in this area are generally suspicious of signing things, and we don't ask until we feel we are trusted.[2]

But if you wish to be entirely safe, it is sound practice to get simple release forms signed at the end of *each* interview.

Storage, Accessioning, and Transcription
Storage
Many sophisticated oral history projects devise elaborate storage facilities for the preservation of their collected material, with a constant temperature of 70° F and a constant humidity level of 50 percent. Most oral history projects in public schools, on the other hand, make no such elaborate provisions. They simply store the collected tapes in file drawers or cabinets, sometimes with the help of commercially prepared storage containers. Other projects have donated their collections to the school library or to a public library or museum in

order to guarantee better storage. As we mentioned earlier, good quality tapes and careful labeling of cassettes aid immeasurably in the storage process.

Accessioning

Accessioning tapes involves keeping track of them in a master index maintained by the project. If you do not plan systematically for the processing of tapes as they are done, they will quickly become overwhelming, like some organism from outer space gone amok! To accession tapes, first be certain that tapes are properly labeled, with interview data sheet and legal release form filled in and signed by all appropriate parties. Some projects print labels to fit on cassette cases to record all of the information of that interview. As tapes are turned in, they should be assigned an accession number, which may simply be a numerical listing of sequential acquisition (although the accession number may also describe number of tapes in that interview, date of interview, or some other data as well). The accession process provides an addition to your list of individuals interviewed and allows you to locate that particular interview if needed. Some storage systems may use nothing more elaborate than a file cabinet, with each file folder containing an interview data guide, legal release, and the interview itself. Other projects have much more sophisticated procedures, depending on the nature of the project and the purposes of preservation. Almost all projects now keep their original tapes, despite the cost involved, feeling that the principal document of oral history is the tape itself. The transcribed interview, if it is made, should still be viewed as a secondary source. The original taped interview should be preserved as an object of historical value in its own right.

As with every other dimension of oral history, the actual practice of storing and accessioning varies considerably from project to project, depending on size, financial resources, and purposes of the project. The primary requirement is that you think, *in advance*, about how you plan to deal consistently with the material being collected, to record the significant data regarding its collection, and to preserve and retrieve that information when desired. Your school librarian can probably suggest a procedure that meets your needs as well as any.

Transcription

Probably the single most difficult aspect of an oral history interview is the transcription process. It certainly is the most dreaded, the least enjoyed. Transcription is slow, painstaking work, requiring a great deal of skill to transform a rambling interview into a coherent narrative. Almost all oral history projects transcribe their tapes in order to make them usable as printed matter.

The majority of projects require interviewers to transcribe their own tapes. While at lower grades this may be difficult, the practice is certainly to be encouraged. Students who listen to their own interviews will naturally become more proficient interviewers; the evidence is clear on that. Some projects allow two students to complete the transcription, which more evenly distributes the transcription burden.

A few projects seek outside assistance. The typing teacher may be a source of great help, especially if your transcription process is viewed as a necessary job skill for typing students. Some of the elementary projects use parent volunteers, who donate their time to convert interviews to typescripts. Professional oral history collections make use of skilled transcribers but few if any school projects permit that luxury. Even if the funds were available, we are convinced that the transcription process is so important as a learning experience for students that it should never be eliminated.

The technical details of transcription are not the intended material of this volume, as much already exists about the process of transcription.[3] However, you should be aware of major issues. One such issue involves literal versus edited transcription. Should your students reproduce the conversation precisely, without alteration, leaving in all the warts and blemishes, the mispronunciations and grammatical errors? Or should the interview be "cleaned up," in order to read better and present a more coherent interview? Most projects take some license with the recorded word, dropping sentences here and there and changing awkward sentence constructions. While professional oral historians may cringe at the liberties taken, you should remember the object of your project: to introduce students to the *process* of history and to produce publishable materials. Because the tape recorded interview remains the primary historical document (not the transcript made from it), no great harm will likely ensue if you allow some liberties in the rendering of a recorded interview to paper.

The only standard to which you must adhere is honesty. Words cannot be invented for someone, or one emphasis ignored while another is added. The obligation of your students is to produce the most accurate record possible, preserving both the words and the flavor of an interview. To do anything less is to render the account false and distorted. Obviously, the line between change for improved understanding and simply change for greater impact is thin indeed.

The transcription process, while tedious and fraught with ethical issues, provides enormous understanding for students about the nature of our language. Grammar is no longer a set of silly rules, arbitrarily applied, but a way to provide readers of words with understanding. Paragraphs, periods, commas all begin to make sense as devices to separate speakers, thoughts, and ideas. If you are an English teacher, the transcription process can be used in conjunction with a grammar unit. If you teach history (or some other course), you may want to invite an English teacher to provide a guest lecture or work with students that are having difficulty.

Asking students to transcribe their own interviews also provides feedback on their interviewing skills. Did they ask open-ended questions, for example, that required more than a yes or no answer? Were their questions thought provoking or simplistic? Did their interviews lead them logically in one direction and fully explore one idea or topic before moving on to another? Did they allow the interviewee to talk, even permit some periods of silence and reflection, or did they jump in to fill every void? Many of the more obvious interview errors can be corrected if students have an opportunity to review earlier interviews. Transcription offers a valuable process for listening to and reflecting on previous efforts.

Conclusion

In the preceding pages we have examined a wide variety of very practical issues for the classroom project. Some of these issues must be faced by all classroom oral history projects; others, such as incorporation, advertising, and printing are most pertinent to projects planning to produce a magazine and are discussed in appendix V. We have covered a broad array, stretching from the choice of tape format to problems of transcription. Yet the most important part of your project in terms of outcomes for students is yet to come, in the often difficult arena of interviewing. The interview situation forces students to interact with and react to their interviewees. Their interviewing skills will either ensure excellent interviews or else transform these occasions into disasters of embarrassed questions, faltering starts and stops, and awkward silences. The interview process, and the teaching of interview skills, is perhaps the single most important dimension of your planning. To that all-important area of interviewing skills, we now turn our attention.

4 / A Model for Fieldwork in Oral History

Unlike documentary forms of historical research, oral history brings the student researcher in touch with living, breathing human beings. It is field research rather than library or laboratory research. A very significant part of the value and virtues of oral history lies in this human contact and in the interpersonal skills that are learned in the process of locating, interviewing, and re-interviewing informants. During the oral history interview, students transcend the gaps that so often lie between the generations. They are far more than passive recorders in the process, because they work with their informants to help them create the most vivid record of the subject under study. As we shall explore at length below, this is an active rather than passive approach to the practice of history. The purpose of this chapter is to offer teachers a detailed, stage-by-stage description of the human side of oral history research, from first contact with the informant to final re-interview. This how-to-do-it account is primarily directed at the classroom teacher, because we assume that most teachers will have had little or no previous experience with fieldwork in oral history and that teachers must be the ones to "translate" this chapter (this whole book, in fact) into terms appropriate for their students. Oral history interviewing is a complex skill that is best approached by way of actual experience, and this is as true for teachers as it is for students. We strongly suggest that teachers begin their classroom program by doing their own exploratory fieldwork in oral history. After two or three trial interviews, the strategies and tactics of oral history research discussed in this chapter will make much more sense and teachers will more clearly understand how to translate these procedures into terms appropriate for their particular classrooms and students. We teach you and you teach your students—it is as simple as that—but in both cases actual hands-on experience is the key.

During the translation process, you should keep several general considerations in mind. To begin with, you should be aware that we have appended a short course and review to the more detailed discussions in this chapter. This multipurpose section (appendix VIII) serves as a summary of the chapter and you may choose to read it first, skipping the detailed discussions until later. In addition, you may turn to it for a chapter summary or review or (last but not least) you may use it as an introductory short course in oral history interviewing for your students. This material may be used just as it is, or it may be incorporated in your own brief course in how to do oral history. That is, and should be, entirely up to you.

But we can at this point make some general recommendations about the training of students in oral history. In the first place, don't put students off by making the interviewing process seem too complicated, by too many rules too soon. The process *is* complicated, of course, but those complications are best taught and mastered in a "learning by doing" approach. Give your students some workable guidelines for conducting the oral history interview and get them out and into the field. Too many rules too soon may make the interview process seem more threatening than it really is, making your students like the millipede that had no trouble at all walking until it read a text about how to do it! Keep in mind that, in one sense at least, students (even grade schoolers) are already highly trained in the basic skills necessary for the oral history interview. They aren't starting from zero, but have a life-long experience in the processes of human interaction. The oral history interview builds on this basic social competence. There is clear evidence that even grade school students can do good oral history.

Furthermore, there are ways to make the initial oral history interview less intimidating to novice interviewers. As suggested by some of the project ideas in chapter 2, students may begin with preliminary classroom practice in interviewing and being interviewed. Once they are beyond that stage, they may choose familiar and nonthreatening interviewees for their first "outside" interviews—grandparents, other family members, peers, neighbors, and the like. Especially timid students may be allowed to play other roles than that of interviewer during the classroom oral history project. These students can work at setting up the interviews, transcribing the tapes, or as editors or photographers. Finally, students' qualms often may be allayed by a research team approach to interviewing, in which students go out in groups of two or three to visit the informant. Assuming the interviewees are themselves not put off by this, there is, after all, considerable safety in numbers.

In general, however, students' initial reluctance to interview should be taken with the same grain of salt as interviewees' initial reluctance to be interviewed (more on interviewee reluctance later). What usually happens is that both parties in the interview quickly become comfortable with the situation and go on to enjoy themselves. For novice interviewer, as for interviewee, it is important to break the ice and plunge in, because both persons are very likely to find their fears unjustified.

Another point: Although students begin oral history interviewing with a basic competence in the interactive social skills required, they can greatly improve their interviewing skills through practice, self-analysis, and feedback. During the actual interview, most inexperienced interviewers become so absorbed in the task at hand as to be oblivious to many of the details of what they say and do, but these details, good and bad, become perfectly obvious when they listen to their tapes. We have found that if this feedback loop is built into the research process, students will naturally improve their interviewing skills as they conduct project research. A great deal of teacher prodding for interview improvement probably won't be necessary, because no interviewers like to be heard making fools of themselves!

So, whichever project idea is chosen, we heartily recommend that students be required to monitor, criticize, and correct their own interviews. To that purpose, we have structured our how-to-do-it chapter in terms of a general model for doing oral history—a model we believe is adaptable for most projects. The model includes the stages of pre-interview research, first interview, analysis of the interview, and re-interview.

Edward D. Ives of the University of Maine has proposed this as the basic *scholarly* model for doing good oral history research, and we suggest it as the basic *instructional* model as well. In this case the minimum for good scholarship is also the minimum for good instruction. Pre-interview research may be simple or complex, brief or lengthy, but it communicates to students the seriousness of the task and assures that they don't approach their interviews with inadequate preparation. It insures that they have thought about the historical information they are after, and have created, as the end product of this methodical research, a detailed interview guide to help them obtain it. After the first interview, the student interviewer listens to the tapes, notes the errors to correct, the points to pursue further, and the holes in the information, and prepares for the re-interview. The feedback loop is complete. It should be apparent that the same procedures that make for good oral history also make for maximal instructional benefits. Our basic model is doubtless not adaptable to all projects and classrooms (you, after all, must be the judge of that), but it is adaptable to many different circumstances. Consequently, our chapter is organized in terms of the four stages of the model— pre-interview research, first interview, interview analysis, and re-interview. These stages of the process of oral history are described in detail and for the teacher, but we believe the basic process is adapt-able for a variety of grade levels and subjects. Once again, the teacher must be the "translator."

Before the Interview: Pre-Interview Research

Several very important things must happen before the first interview can take place. These pre-interview stages are (1) deciding on a proj-ect, (2) conducting background research and preparing an "interview guide," (3) locating potentially good interviewees, and (4) screening the interviewees, explaining the project, and setting up the first inter-view. Each of these stages will be considered in turn.

The first task, of course, is to decide on a project. Many possible projects are described in our ideas chapter, but here it seems useful to present our step-by-step discussions in terms of one hypothetical project in social history that may be of some interest to practicing teachers—a study of the old common schools and how they func-tioned. The one-, two-, or three-room common schools were located in the common school districts, which once made up the county school system. A century ago in urban counties and a scant three decades ago in rural ones, most teachers taught in and most students attended these county schools. Every small crossroads community had its own school, and the county was divided into anywhere from ten to one hundred common school districts, each of which was ad-ministered by an elected board of school trustees watched over at a distance by a county school superintendent. This, then, was the county system, and it was from this system that the independent school districts in the larger communities were "independent."

What was it like to attend and to teach in these multigraded, one- or two-room schools? We have almost waited too long to find out. Were there advantages as well as obvious disadvantages to this "lost world" in our educational history? Few documents record what went on in the common schools, and teachers, often faced with sev-eral grades and several subject preparations within a single class-room, seldom found time to write lengthy memoirs. Documentary evidence is thin and artifactual evidence is largely nonexistent be-cause most of the common school buildings were torn down long ago, but the evidence from the living memories of former students and teachers can still be recorded. Daily life in the common school is a perfect subject for oral history. Let us assume that our social studies teacher and his students choose to undertake an oral history study of the one- and two-room common schools in their home county. Teacher and students have decided that they wish to reconstruct the details of daily existence in the county schools: teaching procedures, instructional materials, problems of discipline—everything that made up the daily round. Now that the topic is chosen, the pre-interview research moves into its second phase: conducting background research and preparing an interview guide.

For both scholarly and instructional reasons, it is important that the project not go off half-cocked. Background research of some kind is always a good idea and it is absolutely essential for preparation of the interview guide that project students will need to conduct their interviews. Basic research usually begins with a study of documentary and oral sources that shed light on the topic. These sources may include (1) textbooks and other scholarly works of history; (2) local histories, family histories, and other local materials in community libraries; (3) old newspapers and other primary documents in community or county archives; and (4) the informal recollections of knowledgeable persons in the locality.

Depending upon the research project, this background research may be brief or lengthy; it may find a great deal of supportive material or almost none at all. But in either case, the background research is a necessary "thinking through" of what the project is about, a conceptualization of the research goals that then is embodied in the project's interview guide. Our hypothetical common schools project perhaps has found enough background material to be useful, but not enough to answer the basic questions. The class now knows many of the names of the common school districts and common schools that once operated in the country. They have discovered a few teachers' daily registers stored in the records at the county courthouse, and these list students' names, grade levels, attendance frequencies, and the like. Certain other county records have given the class some idea of school finances, and students have located a female teacher's contract from forty years before that specifies (among other things) that the teacher is "not to ride in a motorcar with any adult male other than her father or brother." A few newspaper articles in the archives of the local paper offer tantalizing glimpses into the internal workings of the local districts (county meets, teacher firings and hirings, etc.), but little more than that. The informal interviews and "asking around" have turned up more detailed evidence and strongly suggest that an adequate number of former teachers and students are alive, healthy, and willing to talk.

At the end of the period of background research, the class prepares an interview guide to aid project interviewers. The interview guide grows out of the research process and represents a topic outline of the historical information the project is interested in obtaining. It is a critical tool for project interviewers but one that they must be careful not to misuse.

The interview guide is a sort of "topical roadmap" of the ground that project students hope to cover during their interviews, or a "shopping list" for the kinds of information they hope to obtain. The interview guide is emphatically *not* a questionnaire from which interviewers will read word-for-word questions. The guide shows that the project has done its homework and carefully planned its research design. It is a necessary tool, but one that must not be abused. Regarding the possibility of abuse, several "don'ts" must be emphasized at this point. The interview guide should be more in the interviewers' heads than in their hands during the actual interview. Interviewers should read and re-read the guide until they have a clear idea of the range of topics the project is interested in. Interviewers should not read from the interview guide, should not check off items as interviewees cover them, and should not allow the interview guide to lockstep the interview. The guide should be in the form of a topical outline only, because word-for-word questions may encourage interviewers to read directly from the guide. Interviewers should keep their primary attention upon the subject of their interview, not the interview guide. Finally, interviewers should not become overly concerned with the sequencing of topics discussed by their informants and disturbed when this sequence departs from that suggested by the interview guide. The interview guide should be logically sequenced, but interviewees are highly unlikely to bring things up in just that order. Sequencing of topics in the interview is *not* that important. Keep in mind, the interview guide is analogous to a shopping list for the historical topics you want to find, and in a real shopping trip, don't you pick up the tomato soup when you come to it, regardless of its position on your list?

So, a good interview guide is a sign that you have done your necessary homework, and it functions in two important ways: it is a shopping list for the kinds of historical information you are after (if you're clear on what you want to find, you are much more likely to find it) and it is proof to the interviewees that you have put in some time and effort, know what you are doing, and are able to ask intelligent questions. In this sense the interview guide is part of making a good impression on the interviewee, and a good impression is central to the process of building rapport.

As a result of its background research, our common schools project has drawn up a detailed interview guide. The guide is designed to be used for interviewing both students and teachers, and the section of the guide directed at former students might read as follows:

Earliest student experiences in the first school attended
Description of early teacher(s)
Attitudes toward school and teacher(s)
Physical description of the school
   External appearance
   Internal layout
   Classroom layout
   Arrangement of desks
   Instructional materials provided
   Cloakrooms, toilets, water
Transportation to the school
Methods of instruction used by the teacher
   Opening of school day
   Methods of instruction
   Teacher adjustments to multigrade classroom
   Grading procedures
   Management and discipline procedures
School/community relationships
   Athletic and/or academic competitions
   Plays, programs, cake walks, box suppers, dances, Friday
      recitations, school closings, etc.
   Other community uses of the school premises
Other common schools attended (follow same topic outline as
   above)

After a similar interview guide is developed, the project is ready to move on to the next stage of pre-interview preparations: the location and screening of possible interviewees.

Quite often, much of this search and screening process may be conducted over the telephone or by informal word of mouth. There are several ways to obtain the names of potential informants. Simply asking around among grandparents and other relatives may work wonders in locating possible contacts. The teacher may ask students in other classes to talk to their families about persons who might be good interview subjects. In addition, teacher and students may write an article or a letter to the editor about their project in the local newspaper, or an announcement on community radio or TV. For example, our common schools project might place the following letter in the letters-to-the-editor section of its community paper. "Dear Sir: The eleventh-grade American history class at Carver High School is studying the old common schools and wishes to contact county residents who attended or taught in the one-, two-, or three-room ungraded schools of rural Carver County. Anyone who attended or taught in such schools or has knowledge of such persons is urged to contact the Carver High School office and leave their telephone number and address."

Other likely sources of information about possible interviewees are the appropriate retired persons' associations (the county retired teachers' association?), senior citizens' groups, local nursing homes, and churches and other community organizations of wide membership. Even posting a brief account of the project on public bulletin boards in post offices, places of business, laundries, and other public places may bring additional interviewees to the project.

The next step is to screen these potential informants to decide which ones to actually interview. Sometimes, if interviewees are limited, the project may disregard the screening step and interview all the possibilities. (The common schools project may find that only twenty or so former teachers are alive and resident in the home county and resolve to interview them all.) More often than not, however, you will locate more possible interviewees than your project has time and resources for. This will require some kind of screening process, often an informal conversation conducted over the telephone.

At this point we must get into the question of what makes a good interviewee. This is not easy to answer, but basically a good oral history informant is someone who (a) *knows* the information, (b) *is willing* to give it, and (c) *is able* to give it. Some potential interviewees simply won't know anything about the topics you wish to explore. Others, probably just a very few, will be disinclined to allow the interview because of distrust of your motives, anxiety about the interview situation, or because "they just don't want to fool with it." Another group has relevant information, is ready to give it, but for various reasons—health, vocal quality, etc.—just cannot make an intelligible recording.

But let's assume that, even after these persons have been eliminated from your list, a considerable number remain. How do you pick and choose among these? How can you tell if a person will make a good informant? Certainly one trap to avoid is the endless quest for the perfect interviewee. As Edward Ives observes,

> the first thing that you have to do in this line of work is to stop looking for that wonderfully gnarled old woman sitting in front of her foxfire in a just-right-squeaking rocking chair and accept the possibility that your neighbor's teen-age son home on vacation from Groton may be a perfect informant. The important thing is to have a very clear idea what it is that you want to find out. Once you know that, you will probably have little trouble in finding good people to talk to.[1]

As a good rule of thumb, several questions answered in the affirmative tend to identify a good informant, for example: Do other persons who both understand the kind of information you are looking for and know this particular person recommend him or her? Does the person's life experience, as revealed in the screening conversation, suggest that he or she would know the information? Does the person clearly understand what you are looking for and believe that he or she can contribute to the study? Is he or she ready and willing to be interviewed, and do they seem confident, talkative, and otherwise "ready to go"? Finally, does the person seem alert and possess a detailed memory?

But at this point an important caution is in order. Be prepared for many potential informants to be unduly pessimistic about their ability to contribute to your project. If the other evidence suggests that the person should be a good informant, take these professions of doubt with some skepticism and remember, as a basic principle of oral history, that informants know much more than they can easily tell. The potential causes for interviewee pessimism include simple modesty (the person just may want you to ask them again), a lack of understanding about what you are after, doubts about their ability to remember, or anxiety about the interview setting itself. All of these problems can be dealt with during the initial contact with the informant. The timid can be encouraged, the nature of the oral history interview can be explained, and fears of being put on the spot can be allayed. Keep in mind that the most familiar form of the interview for many persons today is that of the adversarial or confrontational interview they see on such TV programs as "60 Minutes." The oral history interview is *not* conducted in that way, and you need to make sure that people understand that.

Another common initial misunderstanding contributing to interviewee pessimism is that these persons may be thinking in terms of some kind of "great man" or "big event" notion of history, sincerely believing that they "just don't know any history." A student in the common schools project may find that a teacher who taught forty years in a dozen rural schools while raising a family of seven believes that she just doesn't have anything to add! Such persons simply need your reassurance that they do indeed have much to add to your project.

A final problem, and a very common one, is that most persons are just not accustomed to prolonged, in-depth excursions into their long-term memories, and greatly underestimate how much they can remember, given optimum circumstances. They literally don't know how much they know, and for them, as for their interviewer, the oral history interview is a sort of descent into the unknown, with neither party being quite certain what will be found. (If we have given you the impression that, despite all these screening procedures, the quest for good informants and good oral history is a bit of a treasure hunt, then you are reading us correctly.)

Assuming that you have talked to the person over the telephone or face-to-face and have decided that they should be interviewed for the project, the next step (and the last step of the pre-interview process) is to explain what the project is doing and to set up the first interview. Explaining the project and getting persons to agree to an interview probably won't be much of a problem, especially for school projects like yours. School assignments, teachers, and students seem to arouse far less suspicion than professional field researchers from outside the community. In explaining the project, your object is to offer a truthful but limited explanation of the research. You don't want to tell interviewees more than they want to know, or to in any way bias their testimony. As a basic rule of thumb, when they are satisfied with your explanations, then stop! You may say something like "We're talking to teachers and students about what it was like in the old one-room and two-room county schools, and we'd like to know what you remember about that." There is no reason to get into such matters as "peer teaching," methods of instruction, or the minutiae of what you are after. Save that for the interview.

It is important, however, that the interviewee be left with a good general notion of the kinds of things you will be interested in. Once they are clear on that, they will think about what they know during the period of time between the screening conversation and the first interview. Many practicing oral historians believe that the best interviews are recorded when both interviewer and interviewee understand what they are seeking, so giving informants time to think about the general topic is almost always a good idea.

One final note: The oral history interview resembles a normal conversation, but it differs in one very significant way, and a way the informant should be prepared for. The interview is a trialogue rather than a dialogue, and the third party in the interaction (listening in for posterity) is the tape recorder. Make sure the informant understands you will be bringing a tape recorder when you come to the first interview. Let them get used to the idea—most people have no real trouble with this after they've had a little time to think about it. Don't just show up with the recorder or spring it on the informant at the last minute. ("By the way, I just happen to have a tape recorder in my car. Why don't I bring it in here?") Few persons will refuse to be interviewed before a tape recorder, but if they should, then you have two options: thank them for their time and find another interviewee or consider taking detailed notes.

The First Interview: Interviewing Strategies and Tactics

Assuming that the fateful day has arrived at last and that you have called on Mrs. Laura Jane Rogers, who taught for twelve years in the one-room Cat Spring School, and have set up the interview in her parlor, then what happens next? She has plied you with cookies and lemonade and evidently spent considerable time digging out such school memorabilia as her hand bell, teacher's registers, photographs, and the like, so that you may see them. Now the initiative is with you. As you begin the interview, you should put the basic who, when, and where of the interview directly on the tape. For example, "This is John Thomas. I'm interviewing Mrs. Laura Jane Rogers at her home in Rogersville. The date is October 16, 1984." Then you begin the interview proper, and a good way to begin *any* interview is to ask several background questions about the informant's family, place of birth, and early life history. This background biography is important information to have on the tape, as well as a good, relaxed, nonthreatening way to get started.

After the background material is recorded, you ask the first substantive question of the interview, a question that goes directly to one of the topics about which you are most interested in getting information. This first question sets the tone for much of what follows and represents something of an exception to our general rule against prepared questions on the interview guide. You probably shouldn't write it out, and you certainly shouldn't read it, but you should have carefully planned what the question will be. The first substantive question is an important pattern-setter for the rest of the interview.

This fateful first question should be one that Mrs. Rogers is sure to know a good bit about, that she will be comfortable with, and that she will have to answer at some length and in considerable detail. The idea is to give the interviewee the ball and let her run with it, and the longer the better. From your point of view as an interviewer, this first question has several purposes. In the first place, it demonstrates to Mrs. Rogers that it is her unique knowledge that will be the subject of the interview. In the second, it shows her that she will be expected to do much of the talking, and gets her going on a topic about which she has much to say (it "greases the wheels"). Third, it demonstrates that you are going to be supportive, not confrontational, during the interview. Finally, last but not least, it gives you plenty of ammunition for subsequent questions, questions linked to the interviewee's point of view. To achieve these purposes you want Mrs. Rogers to talk at length and without interruption for several minutes.

This fateful first substantive question is a critical beginning for the interview and a good introduction to the general strategy for doing oral history embodied in this chapter. Let's suppose that you have asked Mrs. Rogers the following question, and then go on from there to a general consideration about the nature of the oral history interview. "Mrs. Rogers," you say, "I know this may sound a little silly, but can you give me an imaginary tour of the Cat Spring School, inside and out, and in as much detail as possible? In other words, what do you remember about external appearance, the arrangement of rooms, classroom layout, positioning of desks and benches, cloakroom and toilet facilities, water supplies, pictures and other wall decorations, textbooks and instructional materials—anything that will help me imagine what the school looked like?"

This will probably take Mrs. Rogers more than a little time to answer, and in that time we would like to make the following points about the strategic (as opposed to the tactical) nature of oral history interviewing.

The oral history interview is a trialogue rather than a dialogue. The tape recorder is the mute third party in the interview and is standing in for historical posterity. This does not mean that getting good sound quality should become the primary consideration in the interview, but it does mean that the needs of the recorder must be taken into consideration. The recorder should be positioned so that your voice and your interviewee's voice are clearly recorded and away from such sources of extraneous sound (noise as opposed to information) as fans, air conditioners, and the like. The testing process for tape recorder function outlined in the preceding chapter should have left you with a good idea of your recorder's capacities. You should respect its needs, because it represents the interests of all the concerned persons who will ever listen to the interview. You owe it to them, and to your informant, to make the most technically competent recording that you can.

We don't mean by this that the tape recorder should come to dominate the interview, to intimidate the informant (and you?), or to lead to such obvious foolishness as "Would you speak a little more directly into the microphone, Mrs. Rogers?" We simply mean that the recorder shouldn't be relegated to the role of a casual eavesdropper on the conversation.

In addition, because this third party in the trialogue is "blind," you must verbalize those portions of the interviewee's testimony initially conveyed by nonverbal means. Mrs. Rogers may say, "Well, the students' desks were about this wide" (holding her hands a certain distance apart) and you will interject, "About three feet, right?" Because the tape recorder cannot see what goes on, you must be sensitive to those occasions when Mrs. Rogers's testimony needs to be made more detailed and visual for her historical audience. Once again, these concerns are unlikely to be misunderstood by the interviewee, who is perfectly well aware that this is a formal interview of sorts. Mrs. Rogers is more likely to be reassured by them as signs that you know what you are doing. Also, you must have proper names of people and places spelled out, letter by letter, before you leave the interview. It is usually better not to interrupt the flow of the narrative, so you may wish instead to jot down names on your note pad as they occur and ask Mrs. Rogers to spell them out either when she reaches an appropriate stopping point or at the end of the interview.

A second strategic point is that the oral history interview follows a cooperative format rather than an adversarial or confrontational format. As interviewer you do not behave like Mike Wallace, assuming that Mrs. Rogers has something to hide, putting her on the spot, giving her little time to think, challenging her interpretations, and in general trying to blow her cool. During the interview, you work with your subject to help her remember the past and to record the greatest quality and quantity of relevant information possible. With this goal in mind, and in full recognition of the uncertainties of the long-term memory, you adopt a role relative to your subject that is nearly the opposite of the confrontational approach outlined above. You are low-key, reassuring, courteous, and attentive—in short, the perfect listener.

So, as a conversation, the oral history interview is much closer to a normal one-on-one interaction than the confrontational interviews we see on TV. That being said, we may begin to examine the subtle ways in which such interviews *are* different from ordinary conversation.

Some of the ways in which the interview is different should have been communicated to the informant by the manner in which you began the interview and asked your first substantive question. For one thing, you are more flexible (and more permissive) than a person in normal conversation. The basic rule of thumb (taking precedence over all of the more specific recommendations covered below) may be stated as "Behave and converse with the informant in such a way as to get the most and best information possible." This is the primary goal, and to achieve it, "Be flexible!" is the first rule of the oral history interview. Given the cooperative nature of such interviews, this ability to be flexible, think on your feet, and play it by ear is the first and most basic requirement.

Being flexible means that you are not much concerned with who is (or seems to be) in control of the interview. Your job as interviewer is to interact with Mrs. Rogers in such a way as to maximize the quantity and quality of historically relevant information recorded on the tape. Hence, you are the facilitator of the process of recollection in your informant. This means different things with different interviewees. It may mean asking a long series of rather specific questions. Much more often, it means the strategic relinquishment of such direct control in order to get the subject to talk.

In a sense the oral history interviewer is both more and less directive than a person in normal conversation. You usually talk less—ideally much less—than Mrs. Rogers. Interviewers vary tremendously in this regard (be flexible, remember?), but all veteran interviewers know that the one obvious sign of an oral history interview gone wrong is too much interviewer talk. It is the historically relevant talk on the part of the informant that the oral history interview is all about. You are technically in control, but you are ready to tactfully relinquish control of topics and sequencing when that seems strategic. Within the ethical parameters of the interview (see appendix IV) and the general norms of behavior (speech, dress, and demeanor) acceptable to both parties in the interaction, you do what you have to do to get the best information.

In the role of facilitator of the process of recollection, the way you come across as an interviewer, your presentation of self, is very important. This ideal interviewer role was touched on above, but it is worth further elaboration. The ideal interviewer is perceived by the informant as friendly, courteous, and nonjudgmental. You make Mrs. Rogers feel free to express her feelings and emotions as well as her facts, and to offer her own interpretations of past events without fear of immediate challenge. Above all, the ideal interviewer is content to listen, and to listen attentively and with great concentration, to what the informant has to say. Being a good listener, and being perceived as a good listener (which is a somewhat different thing), is the most important part of the interviewer's role. This means several things. It means a strategic shutting of your mouth so the subject of the interview can talk. This sounds very simple, but the personal experience of the authors suggests that it is not always so easy! Being a good listener also means encouraging the interviewee to speak further by smiles and nods of encouragement. It means such interactional specifics as maintaining good eye contact, leaning toward your speaker rather than away from her, and avoiding such obvious signs of nervousness, discourtesy, or inattention as looking more at your notes than at the speaker, drumming your fingers or feet, or looking impatient or bored.

In short, the ideal oral history interviewer not only *is* a good listener, but *looks* like a good listener. Experienced interviewers know just how critical this aspect of their role is, and they cultivate the necessary skills. Many of us initially are not too proficient at playing this good listener role, but it is a very profitable role to cultivate. For both students and teachers, being a good listener has many payoffs in everyday life, and its importance for the oral history interview is hard to overestimate. To sum up, the way you come across, your performance of the interviewer role as a courteous, low-key, supportive, and attentive listener, is one of the basic strategies for getting more and better information.

Another strategic way to look at the interview (and one already touched upon in the discussion of the first substantive question) is as a process whereby you "educate" Mrs. Rogers about the special nature of the oral history interview, thus getting around several "blocking assumptions" that stand in the way of obtaining more and better information.

This really is rather obvious once you begin to think about it. Assuming Mrs. Rogers doesn't approach her interview with the expectation that she is about to be interrogated rather than interviewed, how is she likely to think about it? She will probably assume the interview to be an ordinary conversation with a tape recorder present, and this, as we have seen, is not quite the case. For one thing, the ideal pattern of the oral history interview is one in which the informant does most of the talking, and this asymmetrical pattern is a departure from the familiar pattern of symmetrical (or reciprocal) conversation in which the participants take turns talking, with each one taking up about half the time. Mrs. Rogers is likely to begin the interview in terms of this symmetrical model of conversation, and your patience, sympathy, willingness to remain silent, and unfailing attentiveness will encourage the interviewee to speak at greater and greater length.

Hence, you educate the informant about the special nature of the oral history interview in the course of the interview itself. You certainly cannot start off with the sort of theoretical matters being discussed here! This would cast a pall of excessive self-consciousness over an interaction that you want to be as low-key, comfortable, and relaxed as possible. This educational process goes on as the interview progresses and gradually gets around the several blocking assumptions with which the informant is almost certain to begin, and which stand directly in the way of getting more and better testimony. These blocking assumptions on the part of the interviewee are that this is a normal, or symmetrical, interaction ("I shouldn't hog the conversation"), that a reasonable amount of detail is all that you are really interested in obtaining ("He won't want to know all that!"), and that you are probably aware of a lot of the information already ("Of course he knows how we taught several grades in the one-room school").

Gradually, as the interview goes on, you show Mrs. Rogers (by your actions far more than by your words) that all these blocking assumptions are false—that you want her to take the lead in the conversation, that you have a bottomless interest in the details of the information discussed, and that you need to have everything explained. The difference that these understandings can make in the depth and richness of the oral testimony has to be experienced to be believed.

Various tactical procedures for the conduct of the oral history interview follow naturally from the general strategic considerations outlined above. Because you want the interview to be low-key and relaxed, you should dress in terms appropriate for the circumstances, but generally on the informal side. Of course, informal may mean one thing to a retired sharecropper in a rural community and quite another to the president of a downtown bank! You shouldn't try to "fake it"; you should stay within your usual range of dress and demeanor but within that range adjust to circumstances.

Questions—their substance, sequencing, and the way they are asked—are the basic tactical tools of the oral history interviewer. We have already emphasized that questions should seem impromptu and natural (no verbatim questions on the interview guide!) and that the first substantive question is the main exception to this general rule. This first question, you will remember, should be one that the interviewee is sure to know a lot about, and one that requires a detailed and relatively lengthy answer.

In a general way, the pattern set by the first substantive question is repeated throughout the interview. Each time the interviewee brings up a relevant topic or you introduce one yourself, ask a small-scale version of the initial open-ended question—another question inviting Mrs. Rogers to explore the new topic in depth and detail. Then follow up on her response by asking additional questions to clarify that response, extend it, and elicit additional details. After Mrs. Rogers has completely described the physical circumstances, inside and out, of the Cat Spring School, you may move on to another topic from the interview guide, perhaps (and this is the ideal) one suggested by the informant herself. "Mrs. Rogers," you might ask, "I noticed that you mentioned the problems of getting to school in those days. I'm curious, just how did you and your students get transportation to Cat Spring School in the 1920s and 1930s? Could you describe that for me?"

Let us suppose that Mrs. Rogers has given you a detailed description of the physical layout of her Cat Spring School and you have used that lengthy testimony to go on to these and other matters in which you are interested. After the interview gets going, try to keep Mrs. Rogers talking by asking "open" rather than "closed" questions. An open question is subject to more than one interpretation and can be answered in a variety of different ways, usually requiring an answer of some depth and detail. A closed question has one definite "right" answer, and often can be answered rather briefly or in a yes or no fashion. Such questions are both necessary and useful, but they do tend to condition the informant to giving short answers. Leading questions, which both ask the informant a question and give her plenty of information about what you want to hear, are a particularly unprofitable form of the closed question. "Don't you think," you might say, "that the old one-room schools worked a lot better than their critics gave them credit for?" "I certainly do!" Mrs. Rogers might reply, but in this case you have rendered her testimony highly suspect. Perhaps this is her true opinion, and perhaps not, but your leading question has gotten you precisely nowhere.

Another questioning tactic has to do with the sequencing of questions and topics within the interview. Once again, to reiterate what we said in the previous discussion of the use and abuse of the interview guide, *the exact sequencing of questions and topics is not important*. The interview guide is much more like a shopping list than a questionnaire. We hope we will get all the items on the list, but the order in which we place them in our shopping basket (i.e., tape recorder) is not functionally significant. The basic strategy of the oral history interview is to be flexible. To insist on a rigid sequence of questions and topics read from the interview guide would be to let this basic tool of our inquiry get entirely out of hand.

There is more than one reason why a rigid questioning sequence is a bad idea. Just as it violates the strategy of flexibility, it flies in the face of the ideal interviewer's role as facilitator and perfect listener and, at the very least, it fails to contribute to the gradual process of rapport building that is basic to the success of the interview. Insisting on a rigid questioning sequence may also mean that you fail to record that part of the evidence that lies in the relationship your informant sees between topics—her notions about what topics are most important, her interpretations of events, and her ideas about what causes what. If Mrs. Rogers wants to move from the topic of "school/community relations at the Cat Spring School" to the topic of "management and discipline," you should let her do so, whatever the topical sequencing on your interview guide. Mrs. Rogers's point may well be that there was no significant discipline problem precisely because, in her opinion, school and community relations were so close. You may or may not elicit that opinion again later if you cut her off when she begins to discuss "discipline" simply because that isn't next on your list.

But the most important reason that it is bad tactics to insist on a rigid questioning sequence has to do with the nature of the long-term memory. Most people simply do not remember in rigidly logical sequences, whether topical or chronological, and if you force them to do so, you seriously restrict the quality and quantity of their testimony. The way the long-term memory works is little understood, even by psychologists, but what is certain is that the interviewee *must* feel free to return to previous topics as additional memories surface. Let us suppose that long into your first interview with Mrs. Rogers she recalls that she has failed to describe to you the contents of her "school trunk," that diverse collection of instructional materi-

als (paid for out of her own salary) that she carried with her from
one country school to another. Now, through some chance association that brought it to mind, she is ready to verbally "unpack" this
long-ago-vanished repository of instructional materials. It would be a
tragedy if she didn't feel free to do this because of your insistence on
some rigid topical sequence.

Once again, the oral history interview is a descent into the thick-
ets of memory, and neither interviewer nor interviewee can be quite
certain what they will find there. Topical flexibility is absolutely essential to the success of this "hunting" process, because no one
knows what sort of beast will spring from the weeds. Remember that
Mrs. Rogers knows much more than she can readily tell. Your job is
to help her tell it, and this often means allowing her (encouraging
her, in fact) to return to earlier topics as additional materials are recollected. The human brain has been compared to a computer, but
the functioning of long-term recall is anything but computer-like.
The long-term memory is not even like a good filing system. It is,
rather, a musty attic full of mysterious boxes, trunks, and fascinating
disarray. When a treasure trove (or a "school trunk") is rediscovered
by your informant, you must be flexible enough, and opportunistic
enough, to let her unpack it.

And during the unpacking of memory, another mystery will
come to light. You will find that persons vary enormously in their
ability to recollect the past, and that there are differences in the
quality, as well as the quantity, of the long-term memory. There are,
it seems, both "verbalizers" and "visualizers." During the interview
process some persons seem to be recalling and restating previously
recounted verbal interpretations of their life experiences. Other informants seem to possess visual memories of past events and are capable of giving detailed play-by-play accounts of these events as they
"see" them happen in the process of remembering.

Our point is that both verbalizers and visualizers must feel free
to return to previous topics or time periods or to jump ahead to
items further along the interview guide. If they don't have this strategic leeway then what Edward Ives calls the "principle of serendipity"
simply doesn't have room to work. Serendipity in oral history interviewing is the accidental discovery of historically valuable information, unanticipated by the interview guide. And the principle of
serendipity needs room to operate.

A final important questioning tactic, really a complex of tactics,
has to do with ways to get more and better information from your
informant. Because of the uncertainties of the long-term memory,

and the natural carry-over from the implicit assumptions that guide normal conversation (the blocking assumptions discussed above), many of our interviewees' initial descriptions of topics and events will be relatively superficial or "thin." Our job is to get more information to "thicken" the data. Some of these initial superficial descriptions are superficial for the very good reason that the informant simply doesn't know anything more about the topic. Other descriptions will be initially skimpy because the informant doesn't want to dominate the conversation, thinks that this is all the detail we want or require (Mrs. Rogers doesn't want to bore you, after all), or because the informant assumes we know a lot about the matter already. These are the blocking assumptions that stand in the way of more and better information, and it is strategic on your part to *assume*, until proven otherwise, that these misunderstandings are the problem, and that Mrs. Rogers knows a good bit more than she is telling.

So, at this tactical level, how do you question the informant in order to get more elaborate information on the topic? Doubtless Mrs. Rogers will speak at greater length and in more detail as the interview goes along, and as she realizes your unflagging interest and bottomless quest for additional detail, but how do you help this process along? One way is by asking for the same general information in a different way and/or context later in the interview. (Note that this suggests another good reason for avoiding a rigid topical sequence in the interview; we must be free of it ourselves!) This is not a simple repetition of an earlier question, which might well irritate the interviewee or make her think you were not listening the first time around, but a tactful restatement in other terms. For example, in your common school study, you may have asked Mrs. Rogers a straightforward question on school management and discipline early in the interview, and she may have given you a general answer. Later, you may raise the general issue again in a different context, perhaps in terms of a comparison between discipline in the one-room school and in the modern schools that Mrs. Rogers's grandchildren attended. Now she is called upon to go over the same general ground and elaborate upon and add to her previous testimony on the subject—to thicken the data.

Will she be able to do this? On this topic, almost certainly. Now, when she thinks about "discipline in the one-room school," new associations come up and previously unremembered incidents are recollected. She is able to add to your information on the topic. A related tactic is to ask the informant to cover the same ground during a subsequent interview, and under these circumstances Mrs.

Rogers is even more likely to come up with new information. Once again, you need to be tactful about this—to ask the question in an altered way, in a different context, or as a request for elaboration on what you've been told already. However you do it, it is important to ask for important subjects to be covered again, and you shouldn't be afraid to do this. Skillfully handled, the "redundant question" is one important tactic for thickening the information.

Another is the "probe," which is anything you do at the tactical level to get more and better testimony. Though we have not treated it as such, the redundant question may be considered as one kind of probe. Another probe (and a very simple and effective one, too) is simply silence. Mrs. Rogers tells you something about the topic and comes to a momentary stop. You remain silent, look interested and expectant, and "wait her out," thereby tacitly communicating something like "Interesting. Now tell me more about that!" Tactical silence is a very effective probe for obtaining additional information, because it both shows Mrs. Rogers that you want more detail and gives her time to think of it. Novice interviewers often must be constantly reminded to use the silence probe, because the natural inclination for many is to rush into any conversational void with a comment or question. Nonetheless, the probe of attentive silence is well worth cultivating.

A related kind of probe (because it is often silent as well) is encouragement. By a verbal statement ("That's interesting!") or by a nonverbal gesture of approval (a nod of encouragement, a smile, etc.), you encourage the informant to elaborate further on the topic under discussion. Again, this simple tactic is often very effective in eliciting additional information. Mrs. Rogers is in an unfamiliar circumstance and needs appropriate cues that she is doing fine, that what she has said so far is relevant and interesting, and that (last but not least!) even more information on the topic is desired. If you are naturally shy and reserved, practice developing the ability to project encouragement to the informant. It *is* important.

Another probe is asking for more detail or clarification. After Mrs. Rogers's first coverage of a topic, ask for more detail or for a clarification of certain details already given (either later in the interview or in a subsequent interview). You might say: "Now, that's a good general account of how you handled classroom discipline problems. Could you tell me some more about how you used your contacts with parents when problems came up?" Such a question is a direct way to tell the informant, "So far so good, but tell me more." The clarification probe asks for additional detail to resolve a seeming contradiction in the informant's story, or just to resolve something you don't yet understand.

A related probe is asking for personalization or particularization of general answers. As Edward Ives has noted, interviewees will often give "they" answers to questions. The informant will say, "Well, the way they usually handled that was to . . . ," etc. The person offers a relatively brief general answer to your question, without too much detail. Often, an effective way to elicit that detail is to ask questions that require Mrs. Rogers to personalize and particularize her generalities. You might say, "Can you describe some specific examples of that?" or "Did you have any instances where that happened to you, or to someone you knew about?" You are simply asking Mrs. Rogers to back up her general descriptions (which may be all she thinks you want) with specific examples, and keep in mind that the most detailed and historically valuable examples are always with those where the informant was personally involved. Mrs. Rogers may have noted that "they" (meaning parents) backed her up on classroom discipline, but if you don't ask her for specific examples, you may or may not record the following story (taken from an actual interview):

> In those days we used the strap. And I had a boy that didn't want to take a whipping, so he went home. Walked out and went home. In less than an hour his mother was back with him. She told me, "Now, here's this young man. I brought him right back here, and you whip him or whatever you want to do, because the children been telling me how he's been showing off down here. Now, you just take him and whip him!"

Similar valuable examples lurk behind many of the "they" answers your informants will give. Learn to seek them out.

Another effective kind of probe is interjecting additional or conflicting information from pre-interview research and asking the informant to react to it. This is not done to challenge Mrs. Rogers or to put her on the spot, but to jog her memory and to get her to react to other persons' statements on the topic to elicit more and better testimony. You may say, "Well, that's certainly one good way to go about reading instruction in a one-room school, but Mrs. Barry Hooper told us that she used to bring *two* grades up to the recitation bench at one time. Did you ever do that?" Note that this offers no direct challenge to Mrs. Rogers's testimony, and however she reacts to the probe it will probably elicit additional valuable detail. These "interjection probes" show the informant that you have done some homework, and are also direct tactical applications of our general rule that informants know more than they can easily tell. After more than a decade of training his *Foxfire* students to be good interviewers, Eliot Wigginton has come to understand this very well. Here are his comments on similar questioning tactics recorded in an early seminar for the Oral History Association.

> What you want an informant to do is get into a topic and then begin to expand, and inside that expansion all kinds of things happen. You try to get the kids to ask the same question in a hundred different ways. You know, "How did you do such-and-such? Well, did anybody else in your family do it any differently?" You keep them beating around inside that topic as much as possible—"Have you ever heard of it being done another way?" Then, if possible, you give the kids some information before they go out on a topic that they can carry with them, like other alternate ways of doing something. For example, we're working on an article now about tanning hides. Well, you can tan hides by stretching them over a barrel. You can rub soda on them; you can rub alum on them; you can rub a mixture of flour and lard on them. You can tan them in ashes and water. You can tan them in chestnut oak bark. You can take the brains out and spread the brains on the back side of the hide. There are a hundred different ways to tan hides. You can try to give the kids some of these alternative methods, and then when someone gives their method the kid says, "Well, I've also heard that if you took the brains you could do it that way. Have you ever heard of that?" And the guy says, "Oh, yeah, sure! My grandfather used to do it that way. . . ." You get a whole new thing opening up in front of you. You've got to make the kid realize that the people that he's talking to know an awful lot more than they're going to give them just through his short questions. They have to keep beating around inside there.[2]

A final probe, somewhat similar to the interjection, is asking for explanation of all unfamiliar nomenclature. Humans are verbal creatures, and a lot of the most important things about Mrs. Rogers's knowledge of the topic under study will be tied up in the special words she uses to talk about it. When the informant uses this special terminology, or seems to be using familiar words in some kind of different way, you should be alerted and should use the "nomenclature probe" to find out just what she means. You may hear Mrs. Rogers talk about a "recitation," "the recitation bench," "a teacher's register," and "a teacheridge," and you should ask Mrs. Rogers to explain what all these unfamiliar words mean. It will probably take somewhat longer to detect a different usage for a term already familiar to you in another sense. Mrs. Rogers's use of "class" may seem self-evident at first, but you may finally realize (perhaps after some confusion) that she is using "class" in a special way. For her, a "class" is the term used to designate that ten-minute period during the hour in which one of her six grades is "up front at the recitation bench." With six grades and seven subjects, this meant a school day of forty-two classes in this use of the term! Strange terms, and seemingly familiar terms used strangely, are often keys to understanding and expanding the most salient parts of your informant's testimony, and the nomenclature probe is an important questioning tactic to remember.

Interviews, like all good things, must come to an end, but there is no hard and fast rule about when to end this first interview. Usually, sometime between forty-five minutes and two hours the interviewee will start to tire. And if you have been doing a good job and really working at your listening and questioning skills, you probably will be ready to quit as well! Interviews are tiring to both parties, and you should be careful not to excessively fatigue your informant or to let things get run into the ground. As the interviewee tires, the interview rapidly reaches a point of diminishing returns and is best postponed until next time, after you have had a chance to review the first tapes and when Mrs. Rogers is fresh again. Most experienced interviewers would agree that more and better material is usually elicited by several short interviews rather than one long one.

One basic argument for an interview model to include a re-interview phase is the simple fact that it is all but impossible to tell if Mrs. Rogers has told you all she knows or if she is only tired. How much more does she know? You often can't tell unless you go back for another interview. And what if you have covered only a third of the topics on your interview guide? Well, bravo! Not finishing your list is a sign of a good interviewer and a good interview.

But, once again, with regards to interview length, the basic rule is still "Be flexible." Some elderly persons will be just getting started at the end of two hours, and an interviewer should be prepared to continue the interview. For this reason, it's a very good idea to bring at least twice as much tape as you think you will need.

Often it is a good idea to end the interview with one or two general, positive, and interpretational sorts of questions—questions of opinion, which, like the very first question in the interview, the informant is sure to be able to talk about at some length. This ends the interview on a positive note, and gives the interviewee an opportunity to fill in any perceived gaps in the testimony. At the end of your interview with Mrs. Rogers, you might say, "Mrs. Rogers, what, in your opinion, were the most important differences between being a teacher in a common school and in a consolidated or 'town' school?" Mrs. Rogers is almost certain to have a variety of ideas on this and will probably answer at some length.

What happens if you want and need an interview with a certain informant but, for whatever reason, you can't use a tape recorder? Are you completely out of luck or is there a way to do oral history without the presence of the cassette tape recorder? It may happen that a person otherwise very willing to talk to you will categorically refuse, for whatever personal reason, to be recorded on tape. Or you may show up at the informant's home with a tape recorder that now magically refuses to function, with a defective tape, or (and this happened to a student we know) with a plug-in recorder for a house without electrical outlets. What do you do then?

One option is to record the interview in field notes. Keep in mind that the recording of orally transmitted history went on for several thousands of years before the invention of the tape recorder. If the information you are after is quite limited and specific, you might write down what your interviewee tells you word for word, but if the testimony is to be more extensive, you will need to adopt some procedure for taking brief notes while in the interview situation and then fleshing them out later. Many interviewers have found that the following procedure works very well and can, after some practice, result in a very detailed and accurate account of what goes on in the interview. The general procedure is as follows: (1) During the actual interview, concentrate on carefully listening to what your informant tells you and jot down the key words and phrases in each paragraph-sized unit of the verbal testimony—the core of what you are told in the informant's own words. (2) Stop the interview when you have gotten all the information you think you can deal with. This will vary with your skill and experience, but will probably be less than an hour's material. (3) Then, flesh out the interview notes in detail as soon after leaving the interview as is practical. Try to reconstruct what the informant told you, using the informant's actual words as much as possible. This is the point at which you convert your cryptic field notes into something approximating what was actually said. For a skilled interviewer, this can be very close indeed, but two hints are in order here: (a) don't talk to anyone else before you do this (and again, do it immediately after the interview) and (b) consider narrating your reconstruction of the interview into a tape recorder for transcription later. (4) As additional materials occur to you (and they almost certainly will), add them to the full interview notes. (5) After your interview notes are in their final form, you can submit them to the interviewee to be checked for accuracy and amend them if necessary.

Tape Analysis and Re-Interview

The general stages of tape analysis and re-interview are a basic part of the model for doing oral history suggested in this chapter and, we believe, are a good idea for most classroom projects. There are several advantages to including tape analysis and re-interview in the process of oral history.

In the first place, no interview and no interviewer is ever perfect; listening to the tapes always reveals a variety of loose ends, confusions, and holes in the information to be corrected in subsequent interviews. Mrs. Rogers may have had so much to tell that she could deal with only a portion of the topics on the interview guide. Even at the time, you may have been aware that your informant's answers were becoming shorter and more superficial, seeming only to touch the surface of what she had to say.

Mrs. Rogers, you will remember, knows more than she can easily recollect—at least at a single sitting. If she knows you are coming back she will continue to think about the issues under study and is almost certain to recall additional information. In the first interview she was "instructed" in the special nature of the oral history interview and in the kinds of detail you were after. Now, in the re-interview, you and Mrs. Rogers can reap the benefits of that educational process. Now she knows how the oral history interview works, and more often than not has a good bit more to contribute.

Several of the questioning tactics for recording additional information on interview topics—for thickening the data—work best at the re-interview stage. Mrs. Rogers can be asked to rediscuss certain key subjects. She can also be asked to produce additional details or clarifications to previous testimony, to particularize general answers, and to explain special terminology used during the initial interview.

You will have caught some of these during the first interview, but there is no way you can possibly have caught them all. Interviewing is too complicated and there is too much to do. You are asking questions, thinking about where you stand on the interview guide, monitoring the tape recorder, and maintaining close attention to the interviewee—giving her verbal and nonverbal cues of attentiveness and interest. For a seasoned interviewer like Studs Terkel, as for a fifth-grade student, there is absolutely no way to get all of this absolutely right the first time. Interview analysis and re-interview are always needed.

What is more, there are instructional as well as scholarly reasons for this. The interview offers valuable training in interactional skills of great practical usefulness to students, but only if they continually analyze and correct their mistakes. Some kind of feedback loop must be built into the process so that it not only results in better and better interviews, but better and better interviewers. Tape analysis of the first interview, whether by the student working alone, or with helpful criticism from teacher or peers, provides the necessary feedback for both kinds of improvement.

Let's assume that the first interview has been completed. An optional first stage in the process of interview analysis is to write up the interview while it is still very fresh in your mind, before you review the tape. Because the interview is a joint product of both interviewer and interviewee, your perceptions and feelings about Mrs. Rogers are important to record—are, in effect, a part of the data. There are good scholarly reasons for the interview write-up, and it is also fine training for your powers of observation, perception, and memory. *Foxfire*, for example, requires its students "when in an interview situation, to look closely at the room/environment of the contact, list all the things [they note] there, and the same day write a full description of the setting using that list."[3] But the interview setting is only part of what may be included in the postinterview write-up. The idea is to describe anything that you wish to remember for the tape analysis and/or re-interview, or anything that you think might be helpful to someone listening to the tapes at a later date. What does this include? James Hoopes has suggested that the postinterview write-up should answer at least the following four questions:

1. How you found the interviewee and who he/she is?

2. How you interpret the impact of his/her general attitudes or frame of mind on his/her response to your particular questions?

3. Your assessment of what your relationship was with the interviewee and its effect on what was said?

4. Your background research and any other checks you made on the accuracy of the oral document?[4]

Do you or your students always need to do an elaborate write-up as the first stage of the interview analysis? Of course not. The interview write-up is an optional part of the oral history procedure we are suggesting. It does, however, communicate to students the seriousness of what they're up to. It makes them feel they are doing serious scholarship and, in the process, teaches them observational and writing skills that will help make them better fieldworkers.

Assuming the optional interview write-up is completed, now it is time for you to analyze your tapes and to prepare an amended interview guide to use in the re-interview. You may do the analysis yourself or with the helpful criticism of other researchers. But whoever does the interview analysis, they are likely to find much food for thought!

While it is difficult to articulate the complex interactional skills involved in conducting a good oral history interview, it is relatively easy to see what one has done wrong when listening to the tape. The process is naturally self-correcting, and it can be embarrassing. Student Pengee Crawford describes his first interview, in which he broke all the rules of interviewing by forgetting to be a listener.

> It was awful. It was an interview on apple cider and I narrated the whole thing. I don't think the guy had a chance to say more than two sentences through the whole thing. It was just me saying, "And now he's doing this . . . And now he's moving over to the cider press and doing that."[5]

Doubtless Crawford didn't make the same mistake again. When you (or Studs Terkel, for that matter) listen to the initial tapes you will probably be struck by a sense of lost opportunities. These often include (1) mistakes caused by taking a too-active role in the interview conversation (e.g., Pengee Crawford); (2) occasions where you were impatient or nervous, intervened, and cut off Mrs. Rogers too soon, hence interrupting a fruitful line of testimony, or else failed to give her sufficient time to think about the question; (3) closed, rather than open, questions that had the effect of shutting down Mrs. Rogers's flow of recollection; (4) multiple, badly stated, or overly complex questions that frustrated and confused her; (5) intriguing lines of testimony that you either missed or failed to follow up on; (6) chronological or topical gaps in the narrative that need to be filled in; and (7) topics of interest that you either didn't have time for or else couldn't work into the first interview.

Again, the process of tape analysis is naturally self-correcting, and you invariably will come from it with a body of detailed notes on what you will correct and explore in subsequent interviews. You may resolve to be more low-key and to wait the informant out on questions, putting aside your impatience. You may plan to ask certain tactical questions, and so invite Mrs. Rogers to fill in gaps in her previous testimony. You may resolve to coax Mrs. Rogers into some of those intriguing "other rooms" of memory that were only hinted at in passing in the first interview.

This filling in of gaps is a natural part of the interview process. Even where an interviewer is very experienced, the oral history interview rarely follows a strictly logical topical or chronological sequence. The long-term memory just doesn't seem to work that way. There will always be gaps in the narrative. Furthermore, the informant must feel free to circle back to earlier periods or topics as additional material about them is recalled. In the course of several interviews, this circling process will greatly increase the body of information on any given chronological period or topic.

From an instructional perspective, the process of interview analysis and re-interview is an important part of doing classroom oral history. It gives you a clear view of what you did right—and wrong— during the first interview, as well as a fascinating chance to listen in on your own interactions and to learn something about yourself. As we have said repeatedly, it is both good scholarship and good instruction. The end product of this process of analysis will be an amended interview guide for the second interview, a second-generation topical shopping list to help you fill in the gaps, obtain more details, correct your mistakes, and extend the information recorded in the first interview. The same general strategies and tactics described for the first interview apply as well to the second and subsequent interviews.

Beyond the Interview: Other Forms of Field Research

The careful reader will have noted that the model of the oral history interview suggested above doesn't seem entirely appropriate for some of the projects suggested in chapter 2. Some field research projects require a less formal approach than the oral history interview. There is, for example, the study of folk crafts such as basket making and quilting. It is very hard to tell someone exactly how to execute these folk crafts, but it is relatively easy to show them how the process works, perhaps even to get them to participate in a hands-on fashion. Likewise, folklore projects that seek to record the forms of folklore as they naturally occur during social interaction use different approaches to fieldwork. These are informal strategies in which the folklorist simply observes and unobtrusively records the folklore as it occurs in its natural context. Oral history may even be studied in an informal, unobtrusive fashion by listening in to the anecdotes, incidents from family history, and "insiders' stories" that are naturally recounted at such occasions as family reunions and holidays.

The oral history interview, it turns out, is just one kind of field research strategy, and this is a good place to get a clear grasp of the alternative forms of fieldwork that may be appropriate for some of the other suggested projects. The common denominators of field research methods (as opposed to laboratory or "experimental" research methods) are the following: (1) personal participation by the researcher in the setting under study, (2) an unobtrusive, noninterfering approach to research, and (3) the use of research strategies and tactics that are transferable to the situations of everyday life.

Field research is done in the field, not in the laboratory, and the field is nothing more or less than the real world. The fieldworker (oral historian, folklorist, or whatever) goes out into the real world to participate in the social setting that is the object of his study, rather than attempting to remove the setting to the lab. The fieldworker participates in the setting in an unobtrusive and noninterfering way to study it, record it, and ultimately describe it from the inside in terms of the insiders' point of view. Because the fieldworker studies the setting as an insider rather than an outsider, his research strategies and tactics are just more careful and elaborate versions of the informal ways of "making social sense" that all of us use all the time. The various questioning tactics of the probe, for example, are often used informally and unconsciously whenever we are conversing with anyone who has information we very much would like to know.

What are the kinds of field research that may be appropriate for projects suggested in chapter 2? To begin with, there is the formal interview, in which the interviewee's comments are carefully recorded on tape or in the interviewer's notes. Obviously, the procedure of oral history interviewing discussed in this chapter falls into the category of the formal interview. This is the kind of field research required by the great majority of suggested projects, hence our emphasis upon it. All oral history research, with the one exception of the natural context study mentioned above, falls into this type.

The next variety of fieldwork is the informal interview, in which the interviewee is aware that he is being interviewed, but no tape recorder is used and no formal notes are taken. Projects where the information is collected by informal conversation with the data written up later in field notes are of this sort. The informal interview is less obtrusive and more "natural" than the formal interview, and is often appropriate for studies in political science or folklore.

In unobtrusive observation the researcher passively participates in the setting under study. He tries to blend into the background and observe what goes on, later recording it in his field notes. The collection of folklore in its natural context by simply "hanging around" in situations where it is likely to be performed (barber shops, teenage talk sessions, etc.) is a perfect example of unobtrusive observation— likewise, it is the kind of oral history study that listens for naturally occurring folk history at family gatherings or reunions. If there is a contemporary one-room school in the vicinity (and there may well be), we could study it by unobtrusive observation. We would simply sit quietly in the back of the classroom observing all that goes on and record detailed notes. The unobtrusive observer may or may not be known as a researcher to all the persons in the setting he studies.

Finally, there is participant observation. The participant observer, as the name implies, is both a more or less full participant in the setting he studies and an observer of the setting; he plays a dual role. For a political science study of a local political campaign, the field researcher might work for his chosen candidate and then write up his field notes later. The fieldworker might study the craft of basketry or quilting (or building a corn crib or a dry stone wall) by actually pitching in and helping out with the process, later carefully recording what he has learned in his field notes. It should be obvious that, of all the strategies of field research, participant observation is the most naturalistic and the least disruptive of the setting. The researcher is a full participant in what goes on, retaining only the commitment to later reflect upon and record his experiences. A participant observer in a one-room school study would be playing the role of either the teacher or one of the students in the teacher's classroom. This may sound a little farfetched, perhaps, but it isn't impossible. Probably one of the most revealing studies of an American public school (in this case, of a large, suburban high school) was made by a researcher who attended the school in the role of student. Phillip Cusick was the participant observer, and his fascinating study was appropriately entitled *Inside High School: The Student's World*. Cusick's work shows the great power of the participant observation approach to fieldwork.

Our book is a text on classroom oral history, not a detailed guide to other methods of field research, but it is a good idea for the teacher to remember that these other approaches exist, that they are scientifically valid, and that they may be appropriate for certain of the projects we suggest in chapter 2. In planning the kind of field research appropriate for a given project the teacher should keep in mind two general principles governing the choice of fieldwork methods. The first principle is that the method, or methods, should fit the research project. This is obvious, but it is worth stating again. The choice of formal interview (oral history interview), informal interview, unobtrusive observation, or participant observation should be based upon the needs of the project. If the subject you set out to study is entirely of the past, preserved only in living memory, then the formal (or oral history) interview is the obvious choice. If the subject of the study is still performed in the present (folklore, folk crafts, politics), you may choose one of the more informal kinds of fieldwork in order to study it as it happens. Why only collect oral history accounts about "plowing with a mule" or "teaching in a one-room school" if we can find examples of those phenomena right down the road? Why not study them in life as well as in memory?

And this introduces a second general fieldwork principle—that, very often for a given project, mixed field research approaches are best. Some projects need a research strategy that combines the formal interview with the more informal approaches of unobtrusive observation and participant observation. In their studies of social history, folklore, and folk technology, the many classroom oral history projects modeled on *Foxfire* have used such mixed approaches to great effect. Students often go out in research teams to study folk crafts such as chair making. One student in the team may begin by interviewing the old chair maker about how he learned his craft, about other old-time chair makers he has known, etc. (the formal, or oral history, interview). At some other time, students might observe and photograph the craftsman as he actually constructs a traditional chair (unobtrusive observation) and they could even join in the process of chair making as actual, hands-on participants (participant observation). As the *Foxfire* magazines demonstrate, these mixed approaches to field research can result in careful, colorful, and detailed descriptions of the topic under study, descriptions that allow readers, should they so desire, to actually replicate the folk craft described.

5 / The Products of Classroom Oral History

Classroom oral history is a process whereby student interviewers and their historical informants create tape documents of lasting personal and scholarly value. The reality of oral history is inherent in the process itself, because even the most modest of classroom projects is creating permanent historical records where no records existed before—transforming fragile human memory into something of lasting value. Very early in the experience of most student interviewers comes the realization that "if we hadn't recorded this, it might have been lost forever."

This sense of "doing real work" is integral to classroom oral history and is the basic explanation of its unique power to motivate students and teachers. Sometimes the materials recorded are of primary interest only to the immediate family of the informant, but other recorded materials are of clear value to serious students of local history and the larger world of scholarship. A year into his "common schools project," our classroom teacher may well discover through background reading or casual contact with scholars at the local university that he and his students have created one of the largest oral history collections on the one-room school in the United States.

Oral history is like that. The possibilities for original research are enormous. Much of American history "from the bottom up" remains to be written, and the public school oral history project is in a strategic position to make real contributions to this process.

In fact, a strong hypothetical case may be made for the school's advantages in this area.[1] Most public schools are adequately supplied with technical hardware adaptable to the purposes of grass-roots scholarship in local history. This includes typewriters, tape recorders, photocopy machines, and cameras and other photographic equipment. Even in rural and small town schools, these technical resources are usually considerable. Likewise, the school's human resources are adaptable to the task. In its teachers, the public school has a cadre of trained professionals in several disciplines who may serve as advisers and consultants to the school-based project. Perhaps most important, the school has the resource of its students— potential fieldworkers in local history—who are personally linked with every social strata and ethnic subgroup within the community. As the field researchers of their own cultural roots, students possess from the beginning a degree of access to community informants that outside researchers might work years to obtain. Clearly, the local school is in a strategic position to make real contributions to creating this grass-roots history.

We called this a hypothetical case, but the general truth of these assertions is really beyond question. At *Foxfire*, *Bittersweet*, *Salt*, *Loblolly*, *Tsa'Aszi*, and hundreds of other places across the country, classroom projects that began as instructional exercises have evolved into enterprises producing magazines, books, and scholarly archives. The tendency is clear, and this, our products chapter, is written in response to it. Very often the modest classroom oral history project evolves into something more ambitious and begins to produce tangible products for school and community.

We will close our book with a discussion of some major project possibilities that teachers themselves have discovered. These evolved forms of the classroom project include (1) the community oral history archive, (2) the *Foxfire*-concept publication (cultural journalism), (3) productions for the local media, (4) community-specific curriculum materials, and (5) historical "problems reports." These are far from the only forms that the developed classroom project may take, but we suggest them as some of the most practical and successful.

We define these ideas for evolved projects (or projects with products) in terms of several common denominators, specifically: (a) the projects are large-scale, affecting the whole school and/or community; (b) the entire class (often several classes) participates in them; and (c) they often have a life that extends beyond a single school year. In the pages that follow, we will briefly describe and discuss these developed projects paying rather more attention to the *Foxfire*-pattern publication, the most successful and widespread form of the evolved project. As in the project ideas chapter, we can't offer the teacher a detailed explanation of how to implement these evolved projects, but we can describe the underlying idea, make some suggestions for getting started, and provide references for further exploration. Like classroom oral history as a whole, these evolved projects are in large measure "teacher inventions," and we will refer you to the real experts on how to do them.

Idea I: The Community Oral History Archive

At many projects, the gradual accumulation of oral history tapes, transcripts, and interviewer notes ultimately suggests the idea of creating a community oral history or folklore archive, located in the school or community library. It is a simple fact that, while many projects initially assume that they will erase their tapes for reuse in subsequent interviews, few of them actually do so. The tapes come to seem much too valuable. As Pam Wood, the teacher-adviser of *Salt*, notes,

> In the interests of economy, several groups have teetered on the edge of erasing the voices of people like Aunt Arie (Carpenter) and Reid Chapman, telling about unique experiences that some of us may never have, unique experiences that may pass from our modern world and *nobody* will ever have again. . . . [But most projects] have backed away from destroying oral records of human experiences that they have collected. They have decided their tapes were living things—the kind you can't put a value on—but certainly worth infinitely more than the money that bought them.[2]

A project's tape collection takes on increasing value with the passage of time. *Foxfire*, with fifteen years of experience, reports many instances of families seeking copies of taped interviews after the contact has died. Once, a three-year-old girl was brought in by her parents to hear the taped interview of her grandfather, who had died before she was born. Likewise, the scholarly value of a project's tapes increases with the passing years. If, as scholar David Russo and others maintain, the grass-roots history of America largely remains to be written, then classroom projects are preserving some of the basic evidence needed for writing that history.

If the project decides against setting up a community oral history archive for its tapes, it should at least investigate the possibility of placing copies of project tapes, transcripts, and interviewer notes in a state or university archive. Students and teachers are likely to find that professional archivists place great value upon the materials they are gathering. Many scholars will share the sentiments of Francis C. Hartgen, former head of special collections of the University of Maine, who wrote in a letter to *Salt*, "I want to encourage you to consider depositing of tapes, letters, notes, etc. collected in conjunction with the project. They ought not to be destroyed but preserved in an institution like ours for future reference and research. The tapes and notes *must* be preserved."[3]

Of course, there is no necessary conflict between the local use of a project's tapes and the needs of scholarship. One set of the tapes might go into a scholarly archive, while another complete set might remain in the community for use by local persons. As suggested before, there are clear indications that local persons will be interested. Many rural or small-town communities are deficient in the raw materials of community history—a "usable past" compiled by and for the community. As Carl Becker has pointed out, the most basic use of history may be to help an individual make sense out of his or her own life by relating that personal experience to the collective experience, and oral traditional history, of family and community.

But traditional history and traditional historians have largely ignored the life of the local community and what Richard M. Dorson has called "oral folk history": "The topics and themes that the folk wish to talk about, the personal and immediate history with which they are concerned . . . the versions of past events that have remained in folk memory and folk tradition."[4] At the community level, Becker's "everyman" generally has had few historical materials with which to work in his search for a usable past, and if he happened to be black or Mexican American (or Cajun or Choctaw, for that matter) he often had nothing at all. Local communities need this usable past—a history that is about them—and it is precisely this sort of material that the oral history archive can supply. As *Foxfire*, *Salt*, and many other projects have discovered, project tapes and transcripts quickly come to be used as an archive by the local community. This is only a step away from establishing the community oral history archive as an evolved project.

The tape archive can be based in the local library or libraries (remember, tapes may be easily copied), perhaps under the joint sponsorship of the classroom project and the local historical society. In its most basic form, the archive might simply be a collection of oral history tapes, carefully labeled with name of informant, date, and topic. Local persons could come in to the library to check them out and listen to them. Alternatively, the project could get much more deeply into the procedures of scholarly archiving of taped materials—indexing, full transcription, and the like. This is no place to discuss the details of oral history archiving, but excellent technical manuals about transcription and archiving are listed in the bibliography. In any case, the community oral history archive is one direction in which the classroom oral history project may evolve. There is clear evidence that something like this is likely to happen anyway as the project's tapes accumulate and as community persons come in to use them. You are likely to discover (as did Pam Wood at *Salt*) that your tapes are "living things—the kind that you can't put a value on."

Idea II: A *Foxfire*-Concept Publication (Cultural Journalism)

Foxfire and the hundreds of oral history and folklore journals derived from its example remain the most common form of the developed classroom project. *Foxfire*-concept magazines are now being published in almost every state in the union, and have played an important role in further spreading the idea of classroom oral history. We sketched the remarkable story of *Foxfire* and its descendants in chapter 1. Now, we would like to briefly discuss some of the issues involved in deciding whether your oral history project will develop into an oral history magazine. (See also appendix V.)

To begin with, let's be more specific about just what a *Foxfire*-concept magazine is. It is a journal of community oral history, folklore, and folk crafts researched by public school students and published for community use—usually sold by subscription, over the counter sales, or both. Such journals are only rarely financed by their schools or school districts (though seed money loans have been fairly common) and usually sink or swim depending upon community acceptance and support. Clearly, that support has almost always been there. Like the oral history archive, the *Foxfire*-concept magazine is another kind of public history, created by and for the local community. The remarkable spread of the *Foxfire* idea against the obvious and recurrent conflicts with the standard operating procedures of the public school and against such instructional countercurrents as back to basics (often defined as standard, rote instruction and nothing but!) speaks volumes about the ability of the *Foxfire* idea to motivate students and teachers and provide local communities with something they really need. Both as instructional strategy and as publishing project, the *Foxfire* magazine *works*; the record seems clear on that point.

A good portion of appendix V, on getting started, is directed at teachers who are contemplating the possibility of publishing a *Foxfire*-concept magazine. We won't repeat that basic discussion here, but will suggest some additional information that teachers may find helpful. In the first place, two excellent how-to-do-it manuals for the *Foxfire* journal already exist, and go into far more detail than we possibly can in this book about such technical matters as transcription of tapes, editing, photography, layout, and magazine production. These manuals are Eliot Wigginton's *Moments: The Foxfire Experience* (1975) and Pamela Wood's *You and Aunt Arie: A Guide to Cultural*

Journalism Based on Foxfire and Its Descendants (1975). Both of these
key works are out of print, but are available in microfiche form from
ERIC.[5] As much as any printed materials can, these works communicate the spirit of cultural journalism and guide teacher and student
through the steps involved in researching, editing, publishing, and
merchandising an oral history/folklore magazine. Two more valuable
sources of information are Eliot Wigginton's introductions in the *Foxfire* anthologies published by Doubleday and *Hands On: The Newsletter of Cultural Journalism*.[6] *Hands On* serves as the general news
exchange for the hundreds of *Foxfire*-like magazines being published
in schools across the country. It contains a great deal of relevant information about the practical side of magazine publishing, as well as
revealing testimonials written by the participants in many different
projects. Other resources are the several book anthologies from student oral history magazines published by Doubleday. These include
the *Foxfire* books 1–7, *The Salt Book*, and *Bittersweet Country*. These
anthologies serve several purposes. They show students and teachers
what is possible and challenge them to respond as did Lincoln King
of the *Loblolly* project in 1972, "As I read, I thought that, if these kids
can do it, Texas kids can do it." In addition, the anthologies provide
many concrete examples of the kinds of research articles that may be
included in your magazine, examples that demonstrate that *Foxfire*
and its kin have developed exciting new forms of popular historiography that have proven highly successful among contemporary Americans. One example is the oral life history, in which informants are
interviewed and re-interviewed and their transcribed tapes edited
into a colorful life story. Another is the folk crafts article, which focuses on some aspect of nineteenth-century folk technology in home,
farm, or shop, and presents it in sufficient detail so that readers may
replicate it themselves. Folklorists and historians have studied folk
technology, but they have never been concerned with describing
these technologies in such a way that readers would actually be able
to practice them. The *Foxfire* journals regularly accomplish this and
with much success. The book anthologies from the journals are full
of examples of both the research topics and the ways to present
them. They are recommended reading.

A final suggestion is that the teacher look at some examples of
student journals in the making and—better yet—personally consult
with a teacher already involved with a cultural journalism project.
Hundreds of *Foxfire*-concept magazines are currently being published (a current list may be obtained by writing the Foxfire Fund,

Inc., Rabun Gap, Georgia 30568). Some journals will probably be located in your home state—perhaps even in your immediate vicinity. If you wish to see your project go in the direction of magazine production, we urge you to go straight to the horse's mouth! Our discussion in appendix V of the practical realities of getting started in cultural journalism is based in large measure upon the testimony of these same project advisers.

Idea III: Productions for the Local Media

If you're thinking of projects to "recycle" the colorful oral history your students have been collecting, keep in mind that there are other alternatives to a magazine format. Does your community newspaper carry a regular column on local history? If so, perhaps its editor will be interested in occasional manuscripts derived from your oral history research. If the newspaper doesn't have a regular local history column, why don't you propose one, to be developed from your project's oral history materials and submitted to the paper on a weekly or bi-weekly basis. This might add hugely to students' excitement about involvement in your project. The topics of the historical column could be the same sort of oral history and folk crafts subjects featured in the *Foxfire* magazines, as well as more conventional forms of history. Perhaps the historical column is a real possibility in your situation, or perhaps not, but it is an exciting project that costs you little to find out about.

What about other kinds of media presentations of your project's work? You could talk to local radio stations about the possibility of an audio equivalent of the newspaper column—a regular program for local listeners on "The Past Still Present," "Voices from the Past: A Program of Oral History," etc.[7] Your students might take excerpts from their most colorful interviews and edit them into master tapes to use on the radio show. This process of tape editing is technically simple, requiring, as a bare minimum, only two tape recorders and a transfer wire. You could prepare a lead-in of musical background and explanation that would serve to introduce each of your shows. The shows themselves could focus on a person (one interviewee covering various topics) or a topic (several interviewees covering one topic).

Listening to oral history tapes can be a moving experience and in many ways it is the most direct relationship to the past we can have short of the time machine. Much is lost when human voices are converted to typescript on a page, but the radio project would be a chance to present oral history "in the raw" and at full power. Once again, this is possibly an exciting extension of your project's work into another media and another valid experiment in devising public history for the local community. What have you got to lose?

Even more ambitious are media projects that would result in your oral history being seen as well as heard. The case study of the Skewarkians project in North Carolina (chapter 2) explored several possibilities in audiovisual media, including the slide/tape show and the super-8 movie. Keep in mind that your students are members of the "video generation" and are perhaps much more comfortable than some of their elders with work in visual media. The slide/tape show, combining edited oral history testimony with photos of the informants telling their stories or demonstrating their crafts and skills, would seem a good place to start. The slide/tape show is cheap to produce, and the technical paraphernalia necessary for production (camera, tape recorder, etc.) are usually readily available at the school. Such shows, skillfully handled, can have great emotional impact. They can be presented at school programs and circulated to community organizations to publicize your project.

Several *Foxfire*-like projects across the country are working with super-8 film or videotape. "Jeff-Vander-Lou" and "Project Blueberry," among others, have done excellent work with videotape. Because an increasing number of secondary schools include videotape programs in their vocational and industrial arts departments, perhaps the school's videotape classes and your oral history project could join forces to produce programs of oral history in this, one of the newest of electronic media. Folk arts and crafts (and the folk artists and craftsmen that produce them) are a natural subject for the videotape production, and the local public TV station may be ready and willing to show them for the community. Farfetched, perhaps, but like many things we've discussed in this book, it's already happening! Several projects produce videotape shows and regularly air them on the local TV. The newspaper column, the radio show, and such audiovisual media as slide/tape, super-8 film, and videotape are real possibilities for the developed oral history project.

Idea IV: Community-Specific Curriculum Materials

In chapter 1 we discussed classroom oral history as a flexible strategy that might be used to make any subject "community-specific"—to bridge the gap between textbook and classroom and the world outside the school. The evolved oral history project might choose to work with teachers in several disciplines to research, record, and create a local studies curriculum appropriate to each teacher's subject. These could be oral history tapes and transcripts that would be used in the classroom to bridge the school-community gap.[8] Vocational arts and home economics teachers would have audio tapes and transcripts to help teach their students valuable folk arts and crafts still practiced in the community. The agriculture class could use materials on traditional agricultural practices, English teachers would have a variety of life history and folklore texts to use in reading and literature classes, and social studies teachers would have a wide range of oral history tapes and transcripts. And keep in mind, this testimony from the community is much more than just local history. Your community is part of the United States and (beyond that) the Great World! Those veterans from World War I are only a few blocks away, and have much to tell your classes about what it was like to fight in the "war to end all wars." Similar oral history testimony can be recorded to link your home community with all the major historical topics covered in the textbooks—the "roaring twenties," the Great Depression, World War II, the 1950s, the civil rights movement, and Vietnam. In each case, the textbook account of a topic can be supplemented by oral history tapes and transcripts that quite literally "bring history home."

So, one logical extension of the modest classroom project is to create (probably with some school support) just this kind of community-specific curriculum. Certainly, such materials have great value for classrooms and demonstrate as no standard instructional materials can the relevance of history to the real world. Certainly also, no one else is likely to come along to create this local-studies curriculum besides the school itself.

And in building this curricular bridge between classroom and community, the fieldwork process is fully as important as the curricular products that result from it. At the heart of the idea of classroom oral history is the process of student fieldwork in the community—a form of experiential education. The classroom-based curriculum project would work best if it was an ongoing affair, continually updating and supplementing the formal curriculum with materials drawn from the living fabric of community social life through the medium of student fieldwork.

In short, creation of an interdisciplinary local studies curriculum is a real possibility for the developed project. It may turn out that the best curricular materials are often school and community specific, and that the tools to create them are already in our (your) hands.

Idea V: Historical Problems Research

All communities have their problems, and many of those problems have deep roots in the community past. These might be issues of land usage, jurisdiction, environment, busing, or a hundred other possibilities; communities usually know what their problems are! In the historical problems report the oral history class uses its research skills to compile and present a balanced interpretation of a community problem—its origins, earlier attempts at a solution, and present differences of opinion about how best to solve the problem. We don't mean by this that the project should presume to resolve the issue, but only that it would use oral history to provide research background (and perhaps some recommendations) to present-day decision makers. Many would agree that the public schools can play this sort of research role in their communities, although they have rarely done so. In many places it is difficult to find an alternative institution that is capable of this kind of in-depth historical research into community problems. The research method of oral history can be a powerful tool for getting at the historical truth and, by doing so, provide great insight for the present.

Again, at a number of classroom projects (it is difficult to say how many) this natural extension of the classroom oral history project is already happening. *Foxfire* has done historical background studies of the problems of clear cutting in national forest lands and local land use in Rabun County, and similar projects are going on elsewhere. These historical background studies seem to be logical extensions of classroom oral history to the problems of the here and now, and an option of increasing significance to Eliot Wigginton, the classroom teacher who began *Foxfire*. Because of Wigginton's importance to the spread of classroom oral history, it seems appropriate to give him the last word about the application of classroom projects to the problems of the present-day community—in this case, the small community of Mountain City, Georgia. *Foxfire*'s research about Mountain City can stand as a prototype for what may go on at many other evolved oral history projects. The historical problem of Mountain City was growth—how to stimulate it and how to control it once it comes—a complex of issues that plagues many American communities. As Wigginton explains,

> We decided to work with Mountain City, Georgia, a town in our country with a population of about 450, and a town that has done little discussion about or planning for the future. Incorporated in 1903, the residents had never had a town meeting. With

the cooperation of the mayor and the city council, we began to work toward having one.

Each of the students chose a nearby town, out of our county, but of similar size. Alone, each made appointments to talk with their town's officials, conducted a series of taped interviews, and took a series of color slides of important features. Then they put together a slide show and script that illustrated how each of the towns had changed over the years, and how each had dealt with that change in different ways and how each had prepared—or failed to prepare—for the future. The question posed by the show to the residents of Mountain City was, "To what extent can and should we be involved now in planning and shaping the future according to what we, as a group, want for our town?"

The students also researched and drew two complete maps, one showing what the town looked like thirty years ago, then another showing each house and building in the town today. They then drew up an announcement of the scheduled town meeting, had it printed, and distributed copies door to door to every house and business in the city limits.

On the appointed evening, nearly a hundred residents showed up. The mayor made some announcements concerning a planned town sewer and water project for which he had been trying to get federal help, and opened the floor to questions. Then the students presented their slide show and the maps. A long discussion followed, culminating in the request for more such meetings. The students organized two more, one of them complete with packets that contained more maps, copies of town ordinances that had been referred to in previous meetings, etc.

By the end of the twelve-week quarter, twenty-four residents had formed a committee to sponsor a townwide cleanup as one small initial form of community action. The cleanup was announced by the students, again through a door-to-door campaign. When it was held, the residents turned out in force to clean up their own yards, clean and mow the sides of every town street, and haul off all the trash they could find. A chicken barbecue and a square dance followed that afternoon. The committee still exists today, and now has students involved in plans for a city park and fountain.[9]

As Wigginton says, a small beginning, but a beginning nonetheless. Subsequent decisions were the proper responsibility of the residents of Mountain City, not the students from *Foxfire*, but the students had effectively used their field research, editing, and writing skills to present Mountain City's residents with a clear view of their recent past and present options. They provided them with the necessary information to decide their own fate, and in the process probably learned far more about town politics, the structure of the city council and its duties, and positive organized town action than they would ever have learned in a classroom. This kind of historical problems research can go on—is going on—in other American communities. Classroom oral history is an active approach to the study of the past and one that leads naturally to real world involvements in the here and now. As Wigginton says, "Such projects can teach students that they can be forces for constructive change—[that] they can *act* responsibly and effectively rather than being always *acted* upon."

Appendixes

I. Sample Release Form

Date _____

I hereby give to (name or school) _____ , for whatever scholarly or educational purposes may be determined, the tape recordings, transcriptions, and contents of this oral history interview.

_____ _____
Signature of Interviewee   Signature of Interviewer

_____ _____
Name   Name

_____
Address

Special Restrictions:

_____

_____

II. Oral History Data Sheet

Interviewee _____

Address _____

Phone _____ (zip)

Date of Birth _____

Place of Birth _____

Date of Interview _____

Place of Interview _____

Interviewer _____

Number of Tapes _____ Interview Status: Completed
                                              In Progress

III. The Oral History Association

The Oral History Association, founded in 1966, is the largest professional organization of its type. Included in its membership are teachers, librarians, archivists, local historians, folklorists, anthropologists, government officials, journalists, and numerous institutions and organizations such as volunteer and professional groups, museums, societies, schools and colleges, business corporations, public and private agencies, and historical organizations of every size. This diverse association is drawn together by a common interest in oral history as a significant method for studying and preserving the past.

Membership in the OHA, available at low cost, is one of the best ways for one to learn about the growth of the oral history movement. Through the publications and meetings of the association, members have access to general articles and scholarly papers, book reviews and bibliographic assistance, news of oral history projects, announcements about funding of projects, and innovations in an ever-changing field. OHA members receive the quarterly *Oral History Association Newsletter, The Oral History Review*, and other mail-outs from the association. Small or large, oral history projects usually find the OHA to be the best place where an exchange of ideas on oral history methods can occur.

For further membership information (applications, dues, etc.) teachers may write:

Dr. Ronald E. Marcello, Executive Secretary
Oral History Association
Box 13734, N.T. Station
North Texas State University
Denton, Texas 76203

SOURCE: Thomas L. Charlton, *Oral History for Texans* (Austin: Texas Historical Commission, 1981), p. 73.

IV. Goals and Guidelines: The Oral History Association

Preamble
The Oral History Association recognizes oral history as a method of gathering and preserving historical information in spoken form and encourages those who produce and use oral history to recognize certain principles, rights, and obligations for the creation of source material that is authentic, useful, and reliable.

I. *Guidelines for the Interviewee*
   A. The interviewee should be informed of the purposes and procedures of oral history in general and of the particular project to which contribution is being made.
   B. In recognition of the importance of oral history to an understanding of the past and in recognition of the costs and effort involved, the interviewee should strive to impart candid information of lasting value.
   C. The interviewee should be aware of the mutual rights involved in oral history such as editing and seal privileges, literary rights, prior use, fiduciary relationships, royalties, and determination of the disposition of all forms of the record and the extent of dissemination and use.
   D. Preferences of the person interviewed and any prior agreements should govern the conduct of the oral history process, and these preferences and agreements should be carefully documented for the record.

II. *Guidelines for the Interviewer*
   A. Interviewers should guard against possible social injury to or exploitation of interviewees and should conduct interviews with respect for human dignity.
   B. Each interviewee should be selected on the basis of demonstrable potential for imparting information of lasting value.
   C. The interviewer should strive to prompt informative dialogue through challenging and perceptive inquiry, should be grounded in the background and experiences of the person being interviewed and, if possible, should review the sources relating to the interviewee before conducting the interview.
   D. Interviewers should extend the inquiry beyond their immediate needs to make each interview as complete as possible for the benefit of others and should, whenever possible, place the material in a depository where it will be available for general research.
   E. The interviewer should inform the interviewee of the planned conduct of the oral history process and develop mutual expectations of rights connected thereto, including editing, mutual seal privileges, literary rights, prior use, fiduciary relationships, royalties, rights to determine disposition of all forms of the record, and the extent of dissemination and use.
   F. Interviews should be conducted in a spirit of objectivity, candor, and integrity, and in keeping with common understand-

ings, purposes, and stipulations mutually arrived at by all
parties.
  G. The interviewer shall not violate and will protect the seal on
      any information considered confidential by the interviewee,
      whether imparted on or off the record.

III. *Guidelines for Sponsoring Institutions*
  A. Subject to conditions prescribed by interviewees, it is an obli-
      gation of sponsoring institutions (or individual collectors) to
      prepare and preserve easily usable records; to keep careful
      records of the creation and processing of each interview; to
      identify, index, and catalog interviews; and, when open to
      research, to make their existence known.
  B. Interviewers should be selected on the basis of professional
      competence and interviewing skill; interviewers should be
      carefully matched to interviewees.
  C. Institutions should keep both interviewees and interviewers
      aware of the importance of the above guidelines for the suc-
      cessful production and use of oral history sources.

V. Getting Started with a *Foxfire*-Concept Magazine

We're assuming you've been involved with classroom oral history for
some time, and now are interested in beginning a cultural journalism
project. How do you get started? Before rushing headlong into such a
publishing project, some very real considerations should first be ad-
dressed. The discussions below derive from the experience of actual
classroom oral history projects, large and small, in all regions of the
United States. This experience offers valuable insights into the successful functioning of the classroom oral history magazine—insights
that are best considered *before* you begin. If you read this chapter
carefully and are still committed to an oral history magazine, your
chances of success are probably quite high.

The problem for many teachers, of course, is that they hear
about the idea of oral history, or see the success of *Foxfire*, and forget
to consider some very practical issues involved in an undertaking
like this. As a result, they often fail, sometimes quite soon after starting. They abandon great plans, not because those plans were unworthy, but because in their excitement they failed to take into
account some of the critical dimensions of *any* oral history publish-

ing project. In our opinion, teachers planning to begin a *Foxfire*-concept journal should carefully consider at least four major issues. These are (1) the nature of the project, (2) the relationship of the project to its school, (3) the relationship of the project to its community, and (4) teacher-student roles within the project. In addition, we will have something to say about such practical matters as incorporation, copyright, advertising, printing, and mailing. Each of these practical considerations will be discussed below.

Nature of the Project

Probably the single most important decision you will make involves the nature of the project you are undertaking. What specific goals do you have in mind? Are you trying to collect, record, and preserve some unique aspect of your area? Do you have a great personal interest in that preservation process? Is there community/school support for your work? Obviously, a project that involves many members of the community, provides for a growth in local pride, and is still relatively noncontroversial, would be an ideal focus. There would be little resistance and much support for such a study. On the other hand, examination of some controversial or tawdry aspect of your area's past would probably tend to alienate and isolate your project from the community whose support you will seek. That's not to say that your selection should be animated solely by concern about local feelings; it is to say that local support (both school and community) is crucial to your success.

Many school oral history projects ultimately involve a publication; indeed, some would claim that a publication is almost essential as a tangible result of student efforts. Assuming you wish to follow the *Foxfire* model and publish, a number of questions must be answered at the onset. What kind of publication are you considering? To get an initial idea of the possibilities, you may wish to order several copies from the publications of existing student magazines to serve as guides. A complete list may be obtained from the Foxfire Fund, Inc., Rabun Gap, Georgia 30568.

How often do you plan to publish your journal? Most oral history projects publish once, twice, or four times a year. At first, you may wish to plan for only one publication and see how it goes. Naturally, publishing will involve a printer. What sources for printing are there in your community? What sources are there in your school system? Some initial contacts with potential printers might save you time and effort later (more on this subject below).

Money seems to be one of the constant problems plaguing oral history publishing projects. Despite all the efforts to publish cheaply, such projects invariably cost money. How might you go about getting started? Selling subscriptions to your magazine might be one way to obtain seed money. As strange as it seems, some projects have sold subscriptions to nonexistent journals and then used the advance money to create the project! *Loblolly*, for one, started in just this way. Other projects have gone to the school board or building principal for initial support, while others have turned to businesses and individuals in the community or to foundations or trusts. To begin a microfilm collection in a school in Texas, one teacher went to prominent members of the community and asked for one-hundred-dollar donations. That effort provided almost $1,000 in start-up money. The old standbys—car washes, bake sales, donkey basketball, and the like—have also provided the initial resources for many projects. In this time of shrinking governmental funding for education and consequent increased demands on private foundations, initial support from a government agency or private foundation is less likely than in the past. You are probably better advised to seek local support. Some very imaginative fund raising has been employed by classroom oral history projects. The project adviser of *Golden Hindesight*, a California magazine, probably speaks for this variety.

> I organized a benefit folk music concert to raise some funds. . . . We had a bottle-and-can collecting contest between rooms at school to raise money for printing. We sold advanced subscriptions, booster certificates and T-shirts with the *Golden Hindesight* logo on them. We distributed brochures asking for donations. The kids went out in our three-town area and canvassed about 240 stores for ads. We have also made folk toys, crafts, and duplicates of old photographs for sale.[1]

With initial money in hand, materials can now be procured. What items do you need to begin an oral history publication? Very few, actually; some tape recorders, high quality tapes, and a minimum of storage and record-keeping materials. If your object is to produce only one publication (at least for now!), most of what you need can be borrowed from within the school or perhaps even from your students. As a publishing project becomes more formalized and established, obviously more equipment will be required.

The point of all this is to jog you to make a few fundamental decisions *before* you get started. Some readers may aspire to one day operate a full-blown, well-financed, publishing project. Others, not willing to make such a long-term commitment of time and energy, will choose to try oral history publication as a one-shot affair. This is up to you. Here, as elsewhere, our commitment is not that everyone must start a great project, but that many more teachers should incorporate oral history techniques into their regular teaching in the ways they deem appropriate. For some, this will be a *Foxfire*-concept journal—the pattern discussed in this chapter—while for others oral history will be only one of many strategies employed during the year.

Relationship of the Project to the School

A good many of the problems of operating an oral history publication derive from the changing relationship between you and the school. Recognize before you begin that what you are proposing is quite revolutionary for a public school: students involved in their own education, going out into the community and bringing their new knowledge back into the classroom, producing a journal of public history for community use—a publication that sinks or swims based upon its own merits. This process often ignores the conventional practices of the standard classroom. The textbook suddenly becomes a reference book, not the exclusive source of information. Students may be noisier in your room than in the classroom next door, which in turn invites the curiosity of colleagues and administrators. Suspicious questions begin to be asked, like "What are they doing in there?"

Your school principal is doubtless a key factor in your project's success, and you should move to enlist his or her support at the very beginning. If not an enthusiastic supporter, the principal should at least be neutral toward your efforts. Benign neglect is far, far better than active antagonism! After all, that administrator is in a key position to offer help in providing release time for project research, the use of school equipment, and protection from the occasional criticism that any new project will attract. Reports from the field suggest that most of the publishing projects currently under way (80 percent) had the approval of their principal. A smaller percentage (14 percent) received a "slight approval." Thus, only 6 percent of currently successful projects operated without at least minimal support from their school principals. This should be sufficient warning to the would-be project adviser—ignore the principal at your peril![2]

The principal should be brought into the planning at an early stage and at least invited to serve on your magazine's advisory group (discussed below in the section on relationship to community). If brought in early and convinced of the value of your project, the principal will be in a key position to protect you from the criticisms of other administrators, teachers, or parents, as well as to provide much needed support. Most of the successful publishing projects report that students work on the project both before and after school, and sometimes even on weekends. Many projects are allowed to use school typewriters, photographic equipment, darkrooms, and extra classroom space. All of these extras are more easily provided if the principal is on your side. Yet we must emphasize that there is no one pattern in common practice at oral history publications around the country. Some projects regularly use school equipment and facilities. Others are allowed only occasional use. Some schools or school districts give financial assistance, while others provide no financial support whatsoever. The key to a successful publishing project remains the faculty adviser. You are the one who must make your project go within its set of unique circumstances.

If you are successful, you may face yet another problem—resentment from other teachers. Let's suppose you've worked hard, convinced your principal, and secured a commitment of support, space, perhaps even funds. Almost inevitably, some teacher down the hall will begin to feel slighted. While there may be little that can be done about this, you should at least be sensitive to the problem. Keep in mind, your colleagues are in a position to offer great help to the project, and in tactfully soliciting this help you may kill two birds with one stone. The journalism teacher can help with layout and printing, the English teacher with editing, the typing teacher with transcription, the art teacher with sketches and artwork, and the photography teacher with magazine photojournalism. These teachers, like your principal, need to feel part of—not apart from—your project.

Can your project become a regular course offering? This is an issue to be considered early. Most advisers report that course credit can be received for work on their oral history publications. You may be well advised to look for specific ways in which students can be tangibly rewarded for their project work. In many cases, course credit is given in either English or social studies, although occasionally such credit has also been offered in journalism, art, photography, or clerical skills. Sometimes a project is so successful that a special course is created for it. As one teacher writes us,

> Our administrator is very supportive of our program. It has created such an interest in "Art" [the teacher's subject] that a new course, "Appalachian Cultures," will be added to our curriculum next year. . . . This project has brought honor to the community and the county school system and the county board of education highly supports it.[3]

The grade placement clearly affects the nature of the publishing project. Most projects currently in existence are found in high schools. Some operate at the middle school or junior high school levels, and a surprising number are located in the upper grades of the elementary school. Obviously, the project is inevitably affected by grade level placement. The problems of the senior high project are very different from those of the elementary project. Both level of sophistication and lack of mobility, for example, are difficulties often encountered by elementary programs, whereas different kinds of problems occur in high schools.

Can you expect release time if your project becomes successful? Regrettably, most of the current project advisers report that there has been no reduction in their load just because of project sponsorship. A reduction of sorts occurs if you can teach your project as one of your regular classes. But for teachers just starting out, and projects yet unproven, we suspect that you will simply have to take extra time and to weave your publishing project into one (or several) of your existing classes. Keep in mind that sometimes, as in the case of the project quoted above, success can drastically alter the original circumstances.

Still, at least initially, for those hoping through their publishing project for some relief from regular teaching, the outlook is not promising. Most cultural journalism publications are produced within the normal scheduling of public schools, and for those critics of cultural journalism who claim that it happens only in special circumstances, nothing could be further from the truth. A project adviser at *06 Time* well summarizes the classroom circumstances under which most projects begin.

> Most of the articles were begun during my English classes, although much of the work was done outside school. We have no period assigned for magazine work, and none of my people have a study hall when I have my one conference period. I carry a full teaching load and, as always, most of my staff is also involved in annual, athletics, band and/or agricultural organizations.[4]

Relationship of the Project to the Community

As suggested in the last section, as project adviser you probably will face some questions from teachers and administrators about this publishing enterprise. That wonderment may quickly turn to criticism in the world beyond the school. After all, you are violating the traditional norm of students sitting passively in their seats while you dispense information. In most oral history projects, the teacher is adviser more than instructor. Students are learning by doing, as they conduct interviews, write stories, and produce an oral history magazine. This activity may create some suspicion among community school watchers, especially if students leave school during regular school hours to do their research. In this era of back to basics, some of the public initially may be difficult to convince that your project has merit. "Why aren't those kids in school?" is a question for which you had better prepare yourself.

How do you, as project adviser, cope with this criticism? As you arm yourself to deal with questions of this sort, you may well wish to re-examine our rationale for oral history arguments from chapter 1. Our purpose was to give you theoretical ammunition for this sort of debate. As we noted then, such theory is sometimes very practical indeed! What, after all, is "basic" about what you are doing? Eliot Wigginton and hundreds of other project advisers would argue that some of the most important communication skills—reading, writing, and interviewing—are learned through oral history publication. Supporters of classroom projects also point out that such projects arouse enormous enthusiasm and interest, involving students as never before in the process of their own education. Finally, supporters suggest that students involved in such projects come to understand much more of their past and recognize the accomplishments of others gone before. What could be more basic than that? All of these arguments and more should be carefully considered before you embark on a publishing project.

Beyond such theoretical justifications, a second source of support for your project can be the parents of your students, who may be fruitfully involved at the planning stages. A letter home, detailing your plans and objectives, might be an important first step. At one project in New Mexico, parents were invited to an evening meeting where a university professor spoke, the film *Foxfire* was shown, and plans for that school's oral history project were detailed. Such efforts help to defuse potential public criticism and recruit positive support from parents.

Another important source of initial support for your project in the local community might be the local historical society or some other group interested in state history (DAR, library committee, museum board, etc.). If these groups are recruited as loyal supporters of your efforts, they may serve not only to deflect public criticism but as sources of money and advice. In turn, your project may be able to provide assistance to the local history groups in cataloging collections, implementing some special research they are interested in, or providing tapes and transcripts for their local history archive. Perhaps you and they could even copublish a special project of some kind.

While many of the current oral history publishing projects have had limited formal relationships with local historical groups, they are probably missing a bet in this. Such relationships can be very helpful. Projects do, however, often use public opportunities to advertise and promote themselves. Students and advisers are often asked to speak before community social and professional groups, and projects often receive favorable coverage in the local media. Community newspapers certainly shouldn't be overlooked as a means of spreading the word about your project. The more favorable publicity the project receives, the stronger its position in school and community.

Of course, the best agent of publicity for your project is the magazine itself—a journal of popular oral history and folklore produced by and for the local community. For most communities, no one else supplies this kind of public history, and a well-researched and well-produced first issue is certain to create many friends and supporters in the community at large. (In fact, experience suggests that most of the touchiness in project-community relations alluded to above will likely come *before* this first issue.) The project should make the most of the publicity value of its first (and subsequent) issues. Complimentary copies should go to contributors, principal, school board members, newspaper editors, and other key figures. Whenever newspapers feature stories on your project, these should be saved for future reference and copies made for individuals highlighted in the stories. Community contacts who were the source of stories for your magazine should always receive free copies of themselves in print. Anything that will show off your project in a favorable light should be encouraged.

A successful device for involving school and community in the operation of an oral history publication is the creation of an advisory board. Such boards usually include some key figure or figures from the school administration, as well as persons from the local community. If a lawyer will agree to serve on the board, any legal issues that arise may be resolved more easily. Advisory groups have eased the labors of many project teachers, and the experience of the adviser of *Looking Glass* (Michigan) may be regarded as typical.

> Several months ago we established an advisory board made up of people in the community who have supported us in the

past. I was amazed at the number of excellent ideas they had for marketing our magazine. I think it's one of the best things we have ever done. As an advisor, I can't tell you how comforting it is to have that tangible support. The board is willing to back me when I ask for money, they are going to critique the magazine, and they are available for consulting on any problem that may arise.[5]

Nature of the Adviser

A teacher contemplating an oral history publication should certainly consider the altered nature of teacher-student relationships within such projects. While the problems contingent upon altered relations between classroom and school and project and community are necessary things to consider before you begin, perhaps the most important thing to do is to take a close look at yourself. Are you sure you want to get involved in a project that profoundly alters the customary role relationships between teachers and students?

As we have tried to suggest at several junctures, the oral history project changes the fundamental learning process that goes on in the public school classroom. No longer are students simply the passive recipients of knowledge dispensed from an all-knowing source (that is, you), but are transformed into seekers of knowledge, formulators of hypotheses, active agents in their own learning. The *Foxfire* project is a classic case in point. At *Foxfire*, students vote on the timing of issues, topic selection, editorial decisions, and the use of project funds—in short, every aspect of the publication. Wigginton, as project adviser, has the same power as any student—a single vote. This student initiative grows out of Wigginton's philosophy that if students are truly to learn, then they must be involved as responsible decision-makers in their own learning. They act, rather than are simply acted upon. This philosophical stance is profoundly at odds with much that we do in school and with many of the ways in which we treat children, whether we are teachers or parents. Cat Stevens, in a popular song, summed up the student's-eye view of the conventional relationship when he wrote, "From the moment I could talk, I was ordered to listen." How do you really feel about allowing students to be active, participating members of your class? Can you deal with students in that altered relationship? Most project advisers report that their relationship with students is more informal than that of other teachers.[6] Are you prepared for that greater informality?

What do project advisers themselves have to say about this? Regarding the more informal relationship within his project, one teacher wrote to us:

I have a closer relationship with all my [project] students. We work together in an atmosphere that is, at the same time, tense and relaxed. We regard each other more as fellow-workers than teacher-student.[7]

Another wrote:

Relationships of students and teachers are much closer than usual. We are together long hours in varying situations out of class as well as in my home. Even in class it is a one-to-one relationship most of the time.

Others emphasized that the newly defined student role required active, experiential learning: "Students are given (and do) adult tasks, competing in a world of adult publications. They *can* fail!"

It gives students the opportunity to select their learning, direct it, do it until it is excellent and see the result of their work as reflected by the readership. It is a real live situation in which they are a vital part. What they do or don't do affects the whole project, which is permanent and established. They have much more responsibility than in any other class, crossing all disciplines. They get away from the classroom and use the community (often as far away as 200 miles) as resources. I could go on.

Finally, many advisers stressed to us the role played by the project in increasing student self-esteem and self-confidence. Bob England of the *Sparrowhawk* project wrote:

This whole business of creating a "sense of worth and value" within the student seems to be at the heart of the issue. Though we are out there preserving a valuable chunk of knowledge, consistently adding to the community's understanding of its heritage, we honestly believe that the real advantage is that we have an inexpensive way to encounter learning on several levels in such a positive manner that kids are not really threatened by non-vicarious variables like teacher's opinions. . . . There is a real threat from all manner of different directions, and it is the mastery of these difficulties which enhances learning and promotes positive feelings of self.

But, you may ask, just who are these project advisers? We know some things about them. The majority are in their thirties, with several years of teaching experience. Many teach social studies or English, although the total range of backgrounds is much broader. Most teacher advisers report student staffs averaging from sixteen to thirty students, although many agree that smaller staffs are more desirable. Most have regular teaching loads, but a sizeable number indicate that the oral history class (or whatever it is called) usually counts as part of that teaching load.

The successful project adviser seems to be a curious blend. On the one hand, the adviser appears to be a driving, task-oriented worker, committed to the attainment of a specific goal and perfectly capable of circumventing (or at least overcoming) mountains of bureaucratic regulations and well-entrenched inertia. On the other hand, that same adviser can allow students to have equal say in what goes on and can effectively restrain his or her own ego for the sake of student participation and involvement. That's probably a narrow line to walk, but many have successfully walked it.

Incorporation

Many project advisers, especially those of projects publishing a magazine, soon ask the question: Should we incorporate? The answer is complicated and depends largely on individual circumstances. The experience of projects already in existence provides little guidance: some choose to incorporate, others not, and even those who have express mixed feelings about the experience. In a recent study, 59 percent of teacher advisers were neutral on the issue of incorporation, while 15 percent voted against incorporation and 26 percent either agreed or strongly agreed with the idea of incorporation.[8]

Incorporation means that you form a legally recognized organization, apart from the school, which is registered by the state in which you reside. As a part of a corporation, you are individually protected from personal liability. At the same time, there are reports that must be filed annually, a board of directors that must be elected, and a set of bylaws that must be written.

There are two advantages to incorporation: greater control and greater eligibility for outside funds. Most projects that incorporate do so to control their own finances and make their own decisions on when and where to spend any funds. Project advisers who argue for this control often claim that financial decision making and record keeping are invaluable learning opportunities that should not be denied students.

The greater probable reason for incorporation is for the freedom provided in the decision-making process. Many project advisers want their students to make editorial decisions, accept or reject stories, and preserve the published material as their own. This grows out of fundamental beliefs about the nature of the oral history project. If students are truly to be educated, they must take adult responsibility for their work. They must not "play" at the work of their oral history project, but should be allowed to participate in it as responsible decision-makers. They certainly shouldn't be treated as the typical student council often is, allowed to make inconsequential decisions in a democratic process with even those decisions subject to administrative review. At the heart of the oral history idea is the notion that students *should* take responsibility, *can* be trusted, and *can* do good work.

The idea for incorporation sometimes grows out of project-administrator conflict. Sometimes school boards and building principals, not understanding the nature of the oral history magazine, are less supportive than dictatorial in their approaches to project activities. That response, while unfortunate, is at least understandable. The oral history project often carves out new relationships between students and teachers, schools and community. Those new relationships are sometimes viewed with suspicion by school administrators and certain community members. In addition, administrators charged with the responsibility for schools' programs are justifiably concerned with activities outside their control for which they are still held accountable.

The other principal reason for incorporation involves eligibility for funds from private foundations. Some foundations have specific limitations against the use of their money for public, tax-supported institutions. The act of incorporation can provide eligibility for a wider array of sources of funding, particularly from the private sector. The instrument that opens up new sources, however, also closes old ones. Government grants, especially title money, are no longer available after incorporation, as they are legally required to be used in public schools. The issue of funding, therefore, as a determining reason for incorporation, revolves around anticipated sources of funding.

The whole issue of incorporation is a thorny one, fraught with possibilities and problems. The greatest difficulty of incorporation, aside from the nuisance and cost of application and record keeping, results from the potential friction and distrust between administration and project. The stories of difficulty in this "organization within an institution" are legion: Pam Wood, of Salt, Incorporated (Maine) lost her job in a disagreement between project and school board. The potential for misunderstanding and distrust is great, requiring that incorporation not be lightly considered.

Perhaps Murray Durst, with wide experience in this matter, said it best.

> Really the question to incorporate or not to incorporate comes down to a judgement call. Where the project sees it important to have participating students learn through having actual control of, and responsibility for, the project's money, incorporation as a nonprofit organization makes sense. If that is not a major concern or interest, or if there is strong opposition to incorporation by school administrators and/or school boards, it is possible to have a good project without incorporation . . . funds.[9]

The process of incorporation involves finding a local lawyer and applying for incorporation. While that process varies from state to state, the procedures are similar. You first form a board of directors, ideally after receiving approval from your school board and principal (in writing, if you think necessary!). The secretary of state is then contacted to determine if the name you have selected is being used by others. Then you will need a lawyer to draw up articles of incorporation. Once approved, your intention to incorporate is usually required to be published in local newspapers, and the articles of incorporation, along with a form application, are then submitted to the secretary of state for approval. The process is sometimes lengthy, and may cost $500 or more, although the principal cost, the attorney's fee, may be waived if you have an attorney who is on the board of directors, a member of an advisory board, or just a friend of the project.

Another issue you will wish to consider, if you have decided to incorporate, is tax exempt status. You can obtain the appropriate application form by calling the local Internal Revenue Service office or one of the toll-free numbers listed in your telephone book or available from 800 information (1-800-555-1212). The tax exempt status is important for you to obtain in order to avoid paying income taxes. Individual states with a state income tax may require a separate tax exempt status application or proof that your organization has acquired federal tax exempt status.

Copyright

The issue of copyright inevitably arises in regard to any printed material published by your project. A copyright guarantees your project the exclusive control of the material it publishes, and the process of copyrighting is relatively simple. To copyright a magazine, journal, etc., you must print the copyright mark (©), the copyright owner, and the date and year of publication on the title page of the magazine. Two copies of the magazine and an application form, along with the registration fee, are then sent to the Copyright Office, Library of Congress, Washington, D.C. 20559. This constitutes copyrighting your magazine. The *Foxfire* staff advises applicants to use the name of the magazine as the copyright owner, rather than an individual (such as the project adviser) or the school.

Often magazines and journals forget to include both the copyright information and the project address and cost of subscription on their title pages. Obviously, subscriptions cannot be filled if a reader is unable to write for one! A sample format for the title page of a student oral history publication, which includes all important information, has been suggested by the *Foxfire* project.

> THE PROJECT is published by Guessville High School students, 100 Question Street, Guessville, ON 22222. Subscriptions are $6.00 a year, single copies $2.00 plus 50¢ postage. Back issues are available on request. No portion of this publication may be reproduced in any form, with the exception of brief excerpts for review purposes, without the consent of the editors of THE PROJECT. Copyright © 1978 by The Project, Inc.

While it may seem presumptuous in an introduction to classroom oral history to deal with the issue of reprints, quite a number of projects have been faced with the ego-enhancing situation of being asked permission to use their printed material. That request ought to be looked at carefully. What is the purpose of the reprint, for example? Is it to make money for someone? Will the reprint possibly cause adverse publicity for your project? If the reprint involves one of your informants, you may wish to obtain that person's permission. You are not obligated to seek it if your legal release is properly filled out and signed, but it is still good public relations. The important point is that requests for reprints should be carefully scrutinized to avoid future problems or embarrassments. Additionally, you should ensure that you receive full credit for the reprint and are given complimentary copies of the projected publication. This is little enough to ask for the privilege of using your material.

Advertising

Advertising is a time-honored means for raising money for your publication, and a number of projects resort to it. Some projects have even sold ads for nonexistent journals, with the promise that both journals and ads would eventually appear!

One difficulty with the selling of ads is that you certainly won't be the first in your school to approach local merchants. The school annual, the football programs, and other school publications probably use ad sales to support their efforts. How can you provide a service that will attract ad customers? One simple strategy is to offer to design the ads at school, using student talent. The art teacher might welcome the opportunity to provide a commercial art experience for his or her students. Locally designed ads can be imaginative and expressive, and community business people might welcome some creative designs. You may want to create a set of ads that suggests an earlier period, a nice accompaniment to your stories of yesteryear. Students may even enjoy researching ads of an earlier period as they design these ads. One oral history project, *Moon Shadow*, which used this technique reported that merchants were excited about the ads, in some cases adopting them for permanent logos.

More importantly, *Moon Shadow* made advertising yet another teaching opportunity.

> Students learn the basic characteristics of commercial art and advertising operations. They come to understand better how and why commercials, ads, and billboards are designed the way they are and the kind of psychological impact they potentially have.[10]

If you do decide to advertise, remember the obligation you assume when you take someone's money. You must check copy for correctness, ask the merchants for approval of new designs, and furnish them with sample copies of the magazine or journal. If you ensure satisfaction with the product, you may have an advertiser for life. If you offend someone the first time you sell ads, you may very well not have a second opportunity.

Printing

The problems of printing can cause more anxiety than a teenager's first date. Most of us don't understand the printing process and are consequently intimidated by it. Yet as hundreds of oral history projects have demonstrated, publications can be successfully completed, even with a minimal knowledge of printing processes.

Most modern printing is done on photo-offset equipment. In such a process, camera-ready copy is prepared, photographed, and a metal or paper plate made from the photograph, which is then used to print the final product. Metal plates, more costly than paper, are also more durable and can be saved for reprinting.

In order to prepare your material for printing, you must first prepare camera-ready copy. That means that you must have everything arranged just as it will appear in the final product. Any smudges you make will show up in the final printing. Some journals prepare pages on the typewriter while others prefer to have their material typeset. Typesetting requires that you provide your printer/typesetter with a clean transcript of your magazine. The typesetter then typesets that into whatever typeface, type size, and width and length of page you desire.

Whether you type your material or have it typeset, the next step is to lay out the entire journal on dummy sheets (sometimes referred to as boards). The layout must be exact, because that is what will be photographed and copied. Those dummy sheets, when completely pasted up, are then referred to as camera ready. The layout not only includes the typewritten or typeset words but photographs as well. You must indicate in the final layout where each photograph will go, making a window the exact size of each photograph out of red acetate. The photographs themselves will be put in place by the printer, in a process known as stripping.

The faculty who are regularly involved in printing activities in your school can be a rich source of information. The school newspaper sponsor, the yearbook sponsor, even the football program sponsor will all have experience in printing in your local area. You may even be able to have your magazine printed within the school. However you arrange it, don't overlook the enormous educational benefits students can derive from being involved in all aspects of printing their oral history magazine.

Obviously, some of this layout work can be done by your students, while other processes are best done by the printer. The recommendation is that you sit down with a reputable printer *before* you ever plan a magazine to determine how much you want to try to do. The more steps in the process your students can perform, the less money you will have to spend, so get estimates from several printers. Some printers are more willing to work with a school group than others. Some will not only provide advice but even offer tours through the plant for your students, or show students how to do pasteups to prepare camera-ready copy.

You should insist upon two things in your dealings with printers: written bids and the opportunity to proof any material that is typeset. We are not implying that printers are a pack of scoundrels, only suggesting that relationships are more open, and less subject to misunderstanding, when estimated printed costs are agreed to in writing before any final agreement is reached. Proofing is an absolute necessity if you intend to put out a quality product. Typographical errors occur and cannot be changed once the presses are in motion! If one precaution is to be sounded about printing, it is this: Printers vary greatly in size of operation, skillfulness, and cost. You must select a printer carefully in order to insure that your magazine is the very best quality. A well-designed, well-printed magazine will sell itself; a magazine of poor quality may destroy your project. The magazine is the way you represent yourself to your parents, school, and community. Take pride in your accomplishment.

Mailing

As the cost of mailing continues to escalate, sending copies of your magazine or journal will soon become an expensive part of your operation, especially if you send your magazines by first class mail. There are two other rates that can also be used, depending on your circumstances: second class and third class. Each is appropriate in some circumstances and not appropriate in others.

Second class mail provides a significantly cheaper way to mail than first class. However, there are some restrictions. Second class mailing status requires that you mail at regularly stated intervals, at least four issues a year (which you determine prior to making application); that you keep a subscription list; and that no more than 10 percent of the total copies will be given away free. A one-time fee is required, an application form from the post office must be filled out, and usually there is a delay while your request is sent to a regional center for classification.

Third class bulk permit is another mail category that you can use. Third class allows more flexibility than second class, in that you can mail whenever you want to (ignoring stated intervals, as in second class). The drawbacks to third class include a yearly fee *in addition to* the application fee. Third class also requires a certain minimum number of pieces mailed each time (separated by zip codes when five or more go to one code number, as in second class). Finally, third class mail does not travel with the same priority as second class mail, although in this era of mail service that may be a false distinction at best.

If you decided not to incorporate, and are thus wholly a part of the school, you may be able to use the school's mailing system and status, assuming it uses second or third class (some small school systems do not use anything but first class mail). If you have incorporated, you must have your articles of incorporation and your tax exempt status from the IRS before applying for either second or third class service.

Deciding whether or not to use second or third class mail status, like so many other dimensions of an oral history project, comes down to a judgment call. Do you have enough mailings yet to justify the cost (measured in time, trouble, and money) of going through the application procedures? Is the limitation of mailing at stated intervals (as required by second class) going to make life unbearable, as you rush for deadlines? Is the added cost (annual fee) of a third class permit worth the flexibility it provides? Can postage be eliminated (or almost eliminated) by requiring in-person deliveries of subscriptions by your students?

We do not presume to know your personal circumstances. What is being reported here is the experience of others, in similar public school settings. Some have selected the second class route, while others have piggybacked their mailing on their sponsoring institution's third class permit. One recommendation is made by many: If you are considering second or third class mail, go talk to your local postmaster. Take along a copy of your magazine (or a proposed copy). Bring a copy of *Foxfire*, or some other oral history magazine, as an example of your proposed mailing. Carefully fill out whatever form is required, and then wait patiently. The process really is not mysterious, although it may seem so to the uninitiated.

Conclusion

These few suggestions are not intended to serve as anything like a complete guide for implementing a *Foxfire*-concept magazine. Rather, they are offered as precautionary statements to help you consider whether to venture into this unknown world. We have seen teachers try and subsequently fail, not fully taking into account the altered nature of teacher-student relationships in such projects or the complex interrelationships between project and school and project and community. Yet those who have succeeded (and they are many now) have succeeded beyond their wildest imaginations and hopes. They have overcome difficulties in unique ways, forging new relationships between students and schools. The learning process that results has been permanently affected by these committed teachers. They have shown all of us what is possible. From first to last, our book is dedicated to their efforts.

VI. Criteria for Evaluating Oral History Interviews

One day a student asked me a very sobering question: "How do you plan to differentiate between interviews?" Like many other instructors I have been in a state of euphoria over oral history as a teaching tool. Unfortunately, little thought has been given to standardizing the evaluation of interviews. We have long assumed that because a student interviews a person who experienced the Great Depression, for example, the interview is automatically worth preserving. The question at this point is whether the profession should develop a set of standards by which to evaluate student tapes and transcripts.

While I quickly formulated an answer that seemed to satisfy this perceptive student, I was left with an unsettled feeling. As I reflected upon his question, several very important reasons came to mind for developing oral history criteria. First, because it is the instructor's responsibility to ascribe a grade, it goes without saying that he should be able to provide a tangible defense of his decision. Second, there is a need to standardize the evaluation process relative to oral history research. Third, to eliminate the element of "surprise," students should be informed of the criteria. By distributing and discussing the criteria beforehand, students become more aware of the exact areas to be evaluated. Fourth, if one intends to develop a repository of student interviews, the criteria can be invaluable tools for judging whether a particular oral history should be placed in the repository. In short, criteria will serve to standardize decisions about the value or quality of student interviews.

The criteria I developed for oral history tapes include seven major categories of evaluation valued at 85 points. Part one simply records the topic or focus of the interview. No point value need be assessed here. Part two establishes whether the student labeled the cassette properly. This enables one to catalog tapes easily for storage. Part three is designed to determine whether the introduction of the tape contains fundamental information for the listener. For example, does the interviewer identify himself and the interviewee? Are the location and date given? Is the interviewee asked to give a brief biographical sketch? This kind of information is vital to the person who is listening to the interview. Part four attempts to standardize the evaluation of interviewing techniques—whether the interviewer uses leading questions or makes biased comments. Part five evaluates interviewing style. If the interviewer uses the "hurry-up" approach, it is quite probable that some significant information will go unrecorded. Instead, the person who uses some well-timed flattery will encourage the interviewee to continue with the recreation of the eyewitness account. Part six is basically an attempt to judge the audible quality of a tape. If an interview is difficult to hear or is not free of distracting matter, i.e., a third party or television noise in the background, it will certainly affect the listening quality of an interview. The last criterion is the instructor's judgment of the historical value of the interview. It is entirely possible for a student to conduct a mechanically proper interview with a person who contributes very little substantive information. Such a performance could still earn a very creditable grade. Conversely, a student could conduct a mechanically weak interview with an outstanding interviewee and as a consequence produce a tape of high historical value. This part helps the evaluator decide whether a below average or average quality tape score nonetheless should be kept because of its historical value.

Criteria for Evaluating Oral History Tapes
(85 points)

Student _____   Date _____

Course Title _____   Course Number and Section _____

  I. *Check topic of student interview*
     Great Depression _____   War Veteran _____
     Immigration _____   Other (Identify) _____
 II. *Is the cassette tape labeled properly?* (4 points)
     A. Interviewer _____   C. Subject of Interview _____
     B. Interviewee _____   D. Date of Interview _____
III. *Introduction of Tape* (6 points)
     Does the Interviewer:
     A. Identify self _____
     B. Give the date _____
     C. Identify interviewee _____
     D. Identify purpose of the interview _____
     E. Identify location of the interview _____
     F. Ask the interviewee for a brief biographical sketch
     _____   _____

 IV. *Interviewing Techniques* (30 points)

KEY	*Always*	*Almost Always*	*Usually*	*Almost Never*	*Never*
	5	4	3	2	1

     A. Does the interviewer ask singular questions?
                           5   4   3   2   1
     B. Does the interviewer avoid asking leading questions?
                           5   4   3   2   1
     C. When necessary, does the interviewer seem willing to ask for
        elaboration?   5   4   3   2   1

    D. Does the interviewer ask questions which elicit extended answers?

              5   4   3   2   1   _____

    E. Does the interviewer avoid making biased comments?

              5   4   3   2   1

    F. Does the interviewer have a good knowledge of the subject?

              5   4   3   2   1   _____

 V. *Interviewing Style* (20 points)

    A. Does the interviewer avoid the "hurry-up" approach?

              5   4   3   2   1

    B. Does the interviewer avoid interrupting the narrator?

              5   4   3   2   1

    C. Does the interviewer seem willing to use some well-timed flattery?

              5   4   3   2   1

    D. Does the interviewer stop and start the tape unnecessarily?

              5   4   3   2   1   _____

 VI. *Audible Quality of the Tape* (10 points)

    A. Is the interview environment free of anticipated distractions?

              5   4   3   2   1

    B. Is the tape free of audible difficulties? I.e., hard to hear, parts
       erased, etc.   5   4   3   2   1   _____

 VII. *Instructor's Interpretation of the Historical Value of the Interview* (15
     points)

Excellent	Good	Fair	Poor	
15-14-13-12	11-10-9-8	7-6-5-4	3-2-1	_____

Length of Tape (Time) _____

                                   Total Points _____

VIII. *Comments*

The typescript criteria, valued at 50 points, are divided into three parts. The first is readability of the typescript. A student must exercise some important judgments in editing an interview for false starts and stammerings and for spelling, names, and dates. The instructor should also judge how well a typescript conforms to the tape. Typescript form, accordingly, is the second category for evaluation. Does the student provide a cover sheet? Are people's remarks identified by proper initials in the margin? Is the typescript indexed for easy accessibility of information? The third and most important category for evaluation ascertains whether a signed release form accompanies the typescript. An interview has very limited value if only the interviewer has access to the recorded material. It is the student's responsibility not only to conduct an interview with a cooperative respondent, but also with one who will sanction the use of the interview by others or stipulate the terms for its utilization.

Criteria for Evaluating Typescripts
(50 points)

Student _____   Date _____

Course Title _____   Course Number and Section _____

I. *Readability of the Typescript* (20 points)

KEY   *Always*   *Almost Always*   *Usually*   *Almost Never*   *Never*
       5   4   3   2   1

   A. False starts and stammering eliminated.
                     5   4   3   2   1

   B. Grammatical form, i.e., punctuation, spelling, paragraphing, etc.
                     5   4   3   2   1

   C. Corrected for names, dates, etc.
                     5   4   3   2   1

   D. Accuracy of the transcription. (How well does typescript conform to the tape?)   5   4   3   2   1   _____

II. *Typescript Form* (15 points)

   A. Cover sheet (5 points)   _____   _____
                              YES   NO

   B. Are the remarks of the Interviewer and Interviewee identified by their initials in the margin? (5 points)

                          _____   _____
                              YES   NO

   C. Is the typescript indexed for significant persons, places, and things? (5 points)   _____   _____   _____
                              YES   NO

III. *Does a release form accompany transcript?* (15 points)

                          _____   _____   _____
                              YES   NO
                                          Total _____

IV. *Comments*

By using these criteria, instructors can make more consistent judgments about oral history interviews and more successfully meet their professional responsibility of being able to justify a grade. The criteria can also serve as a basis for discussing with students the strengths and weaknesses of their interviews. Most importantly, they will enable oral historians to begin establishing a standard by which to judge the mounds of taped interviews produced by students.

SOURCE: Frank J. Fonsino, "Criteria for Evaluating Oral History Interviews," *The History Teacher* 13, no. 2 (February 1980): 234–244.

VII. Footnote and Bibliography Styles for Oral Interviews

Library of Congress Style
Footnote

    ¹Muckleroy, Leo. *Oral Interview with Leo Muckleroy*, taped transcript of a tape-recorded interview conducted by student Christine Tinkle, the Loblolly project, Gary High School, (Gary, Texas, 1977) 8p. In the Loblolly archive, Gary High School, Gary, Texas.

Bibliography

Muckleroy, Leo. *Oral Interview with Leo Muckleroy*, taped transcript of a
    tape-recorded interview conducted by student Christine Tinkle, the Lob-
    lolly project, Gary High School, (Gary, Texas, 1977) 8p. In the Loblolly ar-
    chive, Gary High School, Gary, Texas.

Turabian Style
Footnote

    ¹Leo Muckleroy, *Oral Interview with Leo Muckleroy*, taped transcript of a tape-recorded interview conducted by student Christine Tinkle, the Loblolly project (Gary, Texas: Gary High School, 1977) 8p. In the Loblolly archive, Gary High School, Gary, Texas.

Bibliography

Muckleroy, Leo. *Oral Interview with Leo Muckleroy*. Typed transcript of a
    tape-recorded interview conducted by student Christine Tinkle, the Lob-
    lolly project. Typed transcript and audio tape in the Loblolly Archive at
    Gary High School. Unrestricted access. Gary, Texas: Gary High School, 1977.

VIII. Doing Oral History: A Short Course and Review

    1. The raw materials of history, the historical evidence, are con-
tained in documentary records, physical artifacts, and the memories
of living persons. Oral history is the process of interviewing living
historical informants to record the remembered past for posterity.
The term "oral history" is also used for the products of that research
process, whether audio tapes or the transcriptions of such tapes.

    2. After you decide on a research topic in oral history, the next
step is to do background research about your chosen topic in textbooks, scholarly histories, local records, and the informal recollec-

tions of community persons. This background research is necessary in order to refine and focus the original research topic idea, to design a workable interview guide for the project, and to choose suitable persons to be interviewed.

3. The interview guide develops out of the initial stage of background research, and is the most basic tool for doing oral history. The interview guide is a topical "shopping list" for the whole range of subjects about which your project is interested in collecting information. Although the interview guide is a basic research tool, interviewers must be careful not to misuse it, that is, they must not (a) write out word-for-word questions or read from the guide; (b) pay more attention to the guide than to the person they interview; and (c) insist that the interviewee cover topics in the same sequence as on the guide. Ideally, the interview guide should be more in the interviewer's head than hand during the actual interview.

4. After the interview guide is completed, the next step is choosing good subjects to interview. Locate possible interviewees by asking around among knowledgeable persons in your community, by putting notice of your project in the local media and other public places, by contacting associations of retired persons and senior citizens, and by contacting other community organizations of wide membership. Choose the subjects to be interviewed from the persons located by this process. A good oral history informant is someone who knows information about the topics in which you are interested, is willing to be interviewed about them, and is able to be interviewed about them (adequate voice, health, proximity to the school). Be prepared for many persons to begin by being unduly pessimistic about their ability to contribute to your project, and take this attitude with a grain of salt.

5. Before you go to an informant's home or office for the interview, offer a brief explanation of what the project is about, the kinds of information it is after, and so forth. Make sure the interviewee understands that you will be bringing a tape recorder to record the interview. Make a firm date for the first interview and keep it.

6. On the date of the first interview, place a brief "who, what, when, and where" directly on the tape. You may do this before you enter the person's home or else when you begin the interview. Start the interview by asking a few general questions about the person's life history and background. This provides valuable information and serves as a good warm-up for the next phase of the interview. At the end of this biographical phase, ask the first substantive question.

7. The first substantive question is the first question you ask that

goes directly to the topic or topics in which you are primarily interested. It should be carefully planned beforehand, and is an important exception to the general rule against verbatim questions. The job of this first question is to "prime the pump," "grease the wheels," get the informant talking, and set the general pattern for the rest of the interview. This should be a question (a) that the interviewee is sure to be comfortable with; (b) that he is certain to know a good bit about; and (c) that he will have to answer at some length. While he answers, avoid interrupting him and encourage the informant to "run" with the question for several minutes. Items that you wish to follow up on later may be jotted down on a notepad as the person talks.

8. After the subject has given his lengthy response to the first substantive question, you can follow up on various aspects of that testimony, asking for additional details, for clarifications, and the like. This same general pattern is followed as you introduce additional topics from the interview guide not covered by the initial discussion. In other words, whenever you open a new topic you ask small-scale versions of the kind of open-ended question with which you began. The general pattern is to ask an open question about the new topic to which the interviewee will respond at length, and then ask a series of follow-up questions to get the interviewee to extend and clarify his response.

9. As an oral historian, your basic goal is to work with your informant to maximize the quality and quantity of historically valuable information recorded on the tape. In keeping with this goal, the most basic rule for doing oral history is to "be flexible."

10. The oral history interview does not resemble the confrontational style of interview familiar from such TV programs as "60 Minutes." On the contrary, the oral history interview is cooperative rather than confrontational, and your task as an oral history interviewer is to help your interviewee remember more and better information—to facilitate his recollection.

11. In keeping with your strategic role as facilitator of the interviewee's process of remembering, as interviewer you try to come across as low-key, relaxed, supportive, and nonjudgmental. Try to say the least and get the most historical information in return. To the greatest extent possible, play the role of the perfect listener.

12. The interviewer is not much concerned with the sequencing of topics discussed by the informant. Your primary concern is the quality and quantity of information recorded, and to increase this quality and quantity you allow the informant to wander from one

relevant topic to another. This permissive approach helps the informant in the process of remembering; increases interviewer/interviewee rapport; encourages the interviewee to return to earlier topics to add additional detail as more is remembered; and is consistent with the interviewer's role as low-key, perfect listener.

13. The informant is likely to begin the interview with the expectation that it is more like a normal conversation than it really is, and you must show him in the course of the interview that these "blocking assumptions" (blocking and limiting the quality and quantity of the historical information) are false. In a normal conversation each person talks approximately half the time, doesn't give a boring amount of detail on any subject, and assumes that the other person already knows a good bit about what is discussed. As an oral history interviewer you must gradually communicate to your informant that you expect him to talk most of the time, that you have a bottomless interest in the details of the topics discussed (you're boredom-proof!), and that you need to have everything explained.

14. A basic assumption you must make as an interviewer is that most interviewees know a lot more information than they can easily tell, and your job is to help the interviewee remember and record the past. Because interviewees tend to regard the interview as an ordinary conversation and because of the uncertainties of the long-term memory, most initial descriptions of historical topics will be superficial or "thin." You must assume that these descriptions can be fleshed out with more detail—that the data can be "thickened"—and use specific tactics to bring this about.

15. The general strategy for the oral history interview outlined above helps to increase the richness and detail of the interviewee's testimony as the interview goes on. Other specific tactics for getting more detailed and thicker testimony are to ask informants the same question in a different way later in the interview (or in a re-interview); use silence and encouragement to get the informant to add detail to a topic; ask for more detail or clarification about what the informant has said; ask the informant to particularize and personalize his general answers; interject additional or conflicting information about the topic from the background research and ask the informant to react to it; and ask the informant to fully explain all unfamiliar terminology in his testimony.

16. The initial interview should end when the interviewee first appears to tire—usually between forty-five minutes and two hours. Don't let the interview go on too long. Remember, as a general rule,

that several short interviews will obtain more and better information than one long one. But here as elsewhere the basic rule is still "be flexible."

17. Although this is an optional step in the process, note taking after the initial interview can be very helpful. Because of the need to play the role of close and attentive listener, you probably took few notes during the first interview—perhaps just a few cryptic phrases to help you remember follow-up questions to ask during a long run by the informant. Now you write up your memory of what went on. This includes the nature of your background research for this particular interviewee; your perception of the informant and of your relationship to him, with special reference to the way that perception and relationship may have affected his testimony; the interview setting, i.e., a description of the physical circumstances in which the interview was recorded; and your thoughts about which topics to cover or to re-explore in the next interview. Because oral history interviews are joint products of both interviewer and interviewee, it is important for you to record your perceptions and feelings about what happened.

18. Carefully listen to your tapes to determine how to revise your interview guide before the re-interview of the informant. An additional interview is almost always needed because no interview and no interviewer is ever perfect, and because without a re-interview you can't be certain the person has told you all he knows. Specific purposes for the re-interview are to cover topics on the original interview guide not discussed in the first interview, to fill in chronological or topical gaps in earlier discussions, to go back over important topics to get more detail and thicken the data, to clarify ambiguities and seeming contradictions in the earlier testimony, and to correct several varieties of interviewer mistakes. All interviewers make mistakes!

19. Throughout the interview and re-interview, keep in mind that the interview is a trialogue, not a dialogue. The tape recorder is the silent (and blind) third party, listening in for historical posterity. This means that you should treat the recorder with consideration, try to create the best tape possible, and verbalize all the aspects of the interviewee's testimony (gestures, photographs, artifacts) that are visual rather than verbal. Every interview is a unique and never-to-be-repeated creation of both interviewer and informant, and the tape recorder represents your historical audience.

Notes

1. Introduction

1. Thad Sitton, *Bringing History Home: Classroom Project Ideas for the Sesquicentennial* (Austin, Tex.: Texas 1986 Sesquicentennial Commission, 1981).
2. *Tsa'Aszi* 3, no. 1 (1977): 5–6.
3. Paul Gillespie in Eliot Wigginton, ed., *The Foxfire Book* (Garden City, N.Y.: Doubleday, 1972), p. 20.
4. George L. Mehaffy and Thad Sitton, "Oral History: A Strategy that Works," *Social Education* 41 (1977): 378–381.
5. Michael Frisch, "Oral History and *Hard Times*: A Review," *The Oral History Review* (1979): 70–79.
6. H. J. Geiger, *New York Times Book Review*, October 20, 1974, p. 1.
7. Barbara Allen and Lynwood Montell, *From Memory to History: Using Oral Sources in Local Historical Research* (Nashville, Tenn.: The American Association for State and Local History, 1981), p. 69.
8. Thad Sitton, "The Descendants of Foxfire," *The Oral History Review* (1978): 20–35.
9. *The Public Historian* 1, no. 1 (1977): 1.
10. Gail Parks, "The Foxfire Concept: Experiential Education in a Rural American Context." Paper presented at the Conference on Education in Sparsely Populated Areas, Aurillac, France, December 1978.
11. Tamara K. Hareven, "The Search for Generational Roots: Tribal Rites in Industrial Society," *Daedalus* 107, no. 4 (Fall 1978): 123–135.
12. Eliot Wigginton, "Foxfire," *Southern Exposure* 5 (1977): 187–189.
13. James Hoopes, *Oral History: An Introduction for Students* (Chapel Hill: University of North Carolina Press, 1979), pp. 41–42.
14. Robert J. Lifton, *Death in Life: Survivors of Hiroshima* (New York: Random House, 1967), p. 27.
15. Thad Sitton, "Bridging the School-Community Gap: The Lessons of Foxfire," *Educational Leadership* 38, no. 3 (1980): 248–250.
16. Carl Becker, *Everyman His Own Historian* (New York: Crofts, 1935).
17. Thad Sitton, "Black History from the Community: The Strategies of Fieldwork," *The Journal of Negro Education* 50, no. 2 (1981): 171–181.
18. Wigginton, *Foxfire Book*, p. 13.

19. Lewis A. Dexter, *Elite and Specialized Interviewing* (Evanston, Ill.: Northwestern University Press, 1970), p. 204.
20. Amelia R. Fry, "The Nine Commandments of Oral History," *Journal of Library History* 3 (1968): 63–73.
21. Thad Sitton, "The Oral Life History: From Tape Recorder to Typewriter," *The Social Studies* 72, no. 3 (1981): 120–125.
22. C. L. Sonnichsen, *The Grave of John Wesley Hardin: Three Essays on Grassroots History* (College Station, Tex.: Texas A&M University Press, 1979), p. 26.
23. Thad Sitton, "Public Schools and Public History," *The Educational Forum* 54, no. 3 (1980): 277–283.
24. More on *Foxfire*-concept journals may be found in appendix V. See also *Mornin' Dew*, Clio High School, Clio, Alabama 36017, and *Streetlight*, Metro High School, Chicago, Illinois 60626.

2. Project Options

1. Ruth Hirsch and Miriam Lewiger, "Oral History: The Family Is the Curriculum," *Teacher* 93 (1975): 60–62.
2. Beatrice Spade, "Americans in Vietnam: An Oral History Project," *The History Teacher* 93 (November 1975): 183–192.
3. Sherrod Reynolds, "Golden Hindesight, Homespun, Lagniappe, et al.," *Teacher* 96 (March 1979): 68–71.
4. Barbara Meyer, ed., "Kaleidoscope 20: Oral History in the Classroom" (Boston, Mass.: Massachusetts State Department of Education, 1980) (ERIC: ED 195 485).
5. Lois Martin, "Oral History: How to Mesh the Process and the Substance in U.S. History," *The Social Studies* 63 (1972): 322–326. For an account of a similar oral history study of the Depression, see Michael H. Ebner, "Students as Oral Historians," *The History Teacher* 9, no. 2 (February 1976): 196–201.
6. Lois Martin, "Kaleidoscope 20."
7. George L. Mehaffy and Thad Sitton, "Oral History Tells Its Own Story: The Development of the Loblolly Project," *The Social Studies* 68 (1977): 231–235.
8. Tom E. Arceneaux, "Learning and Lagniappe in Louisiana," *Childhood Education* 54, no. 5 (March 1978): 238–241. See also Reynolds, "Golden Hindesight."
9. Deborah Insell, "Foxfire in the City," *English Journal* 64 (September 1975): 36–38.
10. R. F. Newton, "Oral History: Using the School as a Historical Institution," *Clearing House* 48 (1973): 73–78.
11. Thad Sitton, "The Oral Life History: From Tape Recorder to Typewriter," *The Social Studies* 72, no. 3 (1981): 120–125.
12. Herb Kohl, "What Was It Like When You Were Young?" *Teacher* 96 (March 1979): 14.

13. B. Lee Cooper, "Oral History, Popular Music, and Les McCann," *The Social Studies* 67 (1976): 115–118.
14. Alex Haley, "Black History, Oral History, and Genealogy," *The Oral History Review* (1973): 1–25. See also C. T. Bennett, "Black Roots: Using Genealogy in the Classroom," *The Social Studies* 71 (March/April 1980): 68–70.
15. Alex Haley, "My Furtherest Back Person: The African," *New York Times Magazine*, July 16, 1972.
16. Thad Sitton, "Windows into Time: Creating an Historic Photograph Archive," *The Social Studies* 70, no. 6 (November/December 1979): 275–280.
17. As a case in point, see A. E. Schroeder, "The Immigrant Experience: Oral History and Folklore among Missourians from German and German-Speaking Groups," 1976 (ERIC: ED 127 836).
18. Thad Sitton, "Black History from the Community: The Strategies of Fieldwork," *The Journal of Negro Education* 50, no. 2 (Spring 1981): 171–181. See also Michael L. Tate, "Through Indian Eyes: Native American Oral History in the Classroom," *Teaching History* 3, no. 2 (Fall 1978): 73–78.
19. T. Harry Williams, *Huey P. Long* (New York: Alfred A. Knopf, 1969), p. xix.
20. Richard S. Tallman and A. Laura Tallman, *Country Folks: A Handbook for Student Folklore Collectors* (Batesville, Ark.: Arkansas College Folklore Archive Publications, 1978); Elaine S. Katz, *Folklore: For the Time of Your Life* (Birmingham, Ala.: Oxmoor House, 1978); Barre Toelken, *The Dynamics of Folklore* (Boston, Mass.: Houghton Mifflin, 1979); and Jan H. Brynvand, *The Study of American Folklore: An Introduction* (New York: W. W. Norton, 1978).
21. Thad Sitton and Jan Jeter, "Discovering Childrens' Folklore: A Primer for Teachers," *Teacher* 97, no. 6 (March 1980): 58–61.
22. Richard M. Dorson, "The Oral Historian and the Folklorist," in *Selections from the Fifth and Sixth National Colloquia on Oral History* (New York: Oral History Association, 1972), p. 43.

3. Technical Matters

1. Edward D. Ives, *The Tape-Recorded Interview: A Manual for Field Workers in Folklore and Oral History* (Knoxville: University of Tennessee Press, 1980), p. 29.
2. Pam Wood as quoted in "Release Forms," *Nameless Newsletter* (now *Hands On*) 2 (Winter 1979): 33.
3. See Cullom Davis, Kathryn Back, and Kay MacLean, *Oral History: From Tape to Type* (Chicago: American Library Association, 1977), or Mary Jo Deering and Barbara Pomeroy, *Transcribing without Tears* (Washington, D.C.: George Washington University Library, 1976), for further specific information about transcription.

4. A Model for Fieldwork in Oral History

1. Edward D. Ives, *The Tape-Recorded Interview: A Manual for Field Workers in Folklore and Oral History* (Knoxville: University of Tennessee Press, 1980), p. 33.

2. Eliot Wigginton in W. Cutler, "Oral History as a Teaching Tool," *The Oral History Review* (1973): 29–35.
3. Eliot Wigginton, *Moments: The Foxfire Experience* (Kennebunkport, Maine: Ideas, Inc., 1975), p. 32.
4. James Hoopes, *Oral History: An Introduction for Students* (Chapel Hill: University of North Carolina Press, 1979), p. 130.
5 Quoted in Pamela Wood, *You and Aunt Arie: A Guide to Cultural Journalism* (Kennebunkport, Maine: Ideas, Inc., 1975), p. 20.

5. The Products of Classroom Oral History

1. Thad Sitton, "Public Schools and Public History," *The Educational Forum* 54, no. 3 (1980): 277–283.
2. Pamela Wood, *You and Aunt Arie: A Guide to Cultural Journalism* (Kennebunkport, Maine: Ideas, Inc., 1975), p. 79.
3. Ibid., p. 80.
4. Richard M. Dorson, "The Oral Historian and the Folklorist," in *Selections from the Fifth and Sixth National Colloquia on Oral History* (New York: Oral History Association, 1972), p. 40.
5. Wigginton's book is document ED 120 089 in the ERIC system. Wood's is ED 120 090. To order these in microfiche form, send 91¢ (plus 35¢ postage) for each to ERIC Document Reproduction Service, P.O. Box 190, Arlington, Virginia 22210.
6. For information about *Hands On*, write the Foxfire Fund, Inc., Rabun Gap, Georgia 30568.
7. A recent example of the dramatization of oral history recordings is "First Person America," a program taken from the Federal Writers' Project oral history interviews of the 1930s. A teachers' guide to "First Person America" was published as an insert to the October 1981 issue of *Social Education* (George L. Mehaffy, *First Person America: A Teachers' Guide*).
   In a personal communication, one experienced folklorist and oral historian has offered some good advice for groups planning radio (or slide/tape show) projects. "I suggest here that if you are planning to use field tapes on the radio, you'll have to pay a whole lot more attention to recording quality than if you are going to use them for listening and transcription purposes. I think local radio programs are a great idea, but the tapes have to be good. The same goes for 'slide/tape' shows. In most of those I've seen, the slides are almost always technically better than the tapes! It's a real problem, but if 'slide/tape' or 'broadcast' is your end, you should keep that end in mind when doing the inteviews!"
8. Thad Sitton, "Bridging the School-Community Gap: The Lessons of Foxfire," *Educational Leadership* 38, no. 3 (1980): 248–250.
9. Eliot Wigginton, ed., *Foxfire 6* (Garden City, N.Y.: Doubleday, 1980), pp. 20–21.

Appendix V

1. Sherrod Reynolds, "Golden Hindesight, Homespun, Lagniappe, et al.," *Teacher* 96 (March 1979): 68–71.

2. Thad Sitton, "The Foxfire-Concept Publications: A First Appraisal" (Ph.D. dissertation, University of Texas at Austin, 1978), p. 92.
3. Ibid., p. 93.
4. Winfred Waller, "Letter to the Editor," *Nameless Newsletter* (now *Hands On*) 2 (Winter 1979): 6–7.
5. Nancy Patterson, "Letter to the Editor," *Hands On* 3 (Spring 1980): 4.
6. Robert D. England, "The Ideal Characteristics of Foxfire-Type Projects as Perceived by Teacher-Advisors" (Ph.D. dissertation, University of Alabama, 1979), p. 65.
7. Ibid., p. 114; Sitton, "Foxfire-Concept Publications," pp. 84–89.
8. England, "The Ideal Characteristics of Foxfire-Type Projects," p. 70.
9. Murray E. Durst, "Letter to the Editor," *Nameless Newsletter* (now *Hands On*) 1 (January 1978): 6.
10. Teddy J. Oliver, "On Advertising," *Hands On* 3 (Spring 1980): 11.

Bibliography

Manuals and Texts on Oral History

Baum, Willa K. *Oral History for the Local Historical Society*. Nashville, Tenn.: American Association for State and Local History, 1974.

————. *Transcribing and Editing Oral History*. Nashville, Tenn.: American Association for State and Local History, 1977.

Charlton, Thomas L. *Oral History for Texas*. Austin, Tex.: Texas Historical Commission, 1981.

Cutting-Baker, Holly; Kotkin, Amy; and Yocom, Margaret. *Family Folklore Interviewing Guide and Questionnaire*. Washington, D.C.: U.S. Government Printing Office, 1978.

Davis, Cullom; Back, Kathryn; and MacLean, Kay. *Oral History: From Tape to Type*. Chicago, Ill.: American Library Association, 1977.

Deering, Mary Jo, and Pomeroy, Barbara. *Transcribing without Tears*. Washington, D.C.: George Washington University Library, 1976.

Epstein, Ellen Robinson, and Mendelsohn, Rona. *Record and Remember: Tracing Your Roots through Oral History*. New York: Sovereign/Simon and Schuster, 1978.

ERIC Clearinghouse on Teacher Education. *Oral History: What? Why? How? Guidelines for Oral History*. Washington, D.C.: The Clearinghouse, 1975.

Gorden, Raymond L. *Interviewing: Strategy, Techniques, and Tactics*. Homewood, Ill.: Dorsey Press, 1975.

Grele, Ronald J., ed. *Envelopes of Sound: Six Practitioners Discuss the Method, Theory, and Practice of Oral History and Oral Testimony*. Chicago, Ill.: Precedent Publishing, Inc., 1975.

Hands On: The Newsletter for Cultural Journalism (formerly *Nameless Newsletter*). Rabun Gap, Ga.: The Foxfire Fund, Inc., 1977 to present.

Harris, Ramon I., and Cash, Joseph H. *The Practice of Oral History, a Handbook*. Glen Rock, N.J.: Microfilming Corporation of America, 1975.

Hoopes, James. *Oral History: An Introduction for Students*. Chapel Hill: University of North Carolina Press, 1979.

Ives, Edward D. *The Tape-Recorded Interview: A Manual for Field Workers in Folklore and Oral History*. Knoxville: University of Tennessee Press, 1980.

Kyvig, David E., and Marty, Myron A. *Your Family History: A Handbook for Research and Writing*. Arlington Heights, Ill.: AHM Publishing Corp., 1978.

Lichtman, Allen J. *Your Family History: How to Use Oral History, Family Archives, and Public Documents to Discover Your Heritage*. New York: Vintage Books/Random House, 1978.

McWilliams, Jerry. *The Preservation and Restoration of Sound Recordings*. Nashville, Tenn.: American Association for State and Local History, 1979.

Mehaffy, George L.; Sitton, Thad; and Davis, O. L., Jr. *Oral History in the Classroom. The How to Do It Series*. Washington, D.C.: The National Council for the Social Studies, 1979.

Neuenschwander, John A. *Oral History as a Teaching Approach*. Washington, D.C.: National Education Association, 1975.

Richardson, Stephen A.; Dohrenwend, Barbara S.; and Klein, David. *Interviewing: Its Forms and Functions*. New York: Basic Books, 1965.

Shumway, Gary L.; Curtiss, Richard D.; and Stephenson, Shirley E., eds. *A Guide for Oral History Programs*. Fullerton, Calif.: California State University and Southern California Local History Council, 1973.

Shumway, Gary L., and Hartley, William G. *An Oral History Primer*. Salt Lake City, Utah: Primer Publications, 1973.

Rallman, Richard S., and Tallman, A. Laura. *Country Folks: A Handbook for Student Folklore Collectors*. Batesville, Ark.: Arkansas College Folklore Archive Publications, 1978.

Tyrrell, William G. "Tape-recording Local History," Technical Leaflet 35, *History News*, May 21, 1966, revised 1973.

Watts, Jim, and Davis, Allen F. *Generations: Your Family in Modern American History*. New York: Alfred A. Knopf, 1978.

Whistler, Nancy. *Oral History Workshop Guide*. Denver, Colo.: Denver Public Library, 1979.

Wigginton, Eliot. *Moments: The Foxfire Experience*. Kennebunkport, Maine: Ideas, Inc., 1975.

Wood, Pamela. *You and Aunt Arie: A Guide to Cultural Journalism Based on Foxfire and Its Descendants*. Kennebunkport, Maine: Ideas, Inc., 1975.

Articles and Essays on Oral History

Arceneaux, Tom E. "Learning and Lagniappe in Louisiana." *Childhood Education* 54, no. 5 (March 1978): 238–241.

Elder, Betty Doak. "Coming of Age . . . History and the Elderly Go Hand in Hand." *History News* 34 (June 1979): 153–158.

Eustis, Truman W. "Get It in Writing: Oral History and the Law." *The Oral History Review* (1976): 6–18.

Harris, J. "Speaking of History: Oral History in the Classroom." *Learning* 1 (October 1978): 72–74.

Kachaturoff, Grace, and Greenebaum, Francis. "Oral History in the Social Studies Classroom." *Social Studies* 72, no. 1 (January/February 1981): 18–21.

Key, Betty McKeever. "Alternatives to Transcribing Oral History Interviews." *History News* 35 (August 1980): 40–41.

Leon, Warren. "New England Teachers Go to the Source." *History News* 35 (September 1980): 11–13.

Machart, Norman C. "Doing Oral History in the Elementary Grades." *Social Education* 43 (October 1979): 479–480.

Mehaffy, George L. *First Person America: A Teachers' Guide*. Boston, Mass.: WGBH Educational Foundation, 1981. (Published as an insert to *Social Education*, October 1981.)

Mehaffy, George L., and Sitton, Thad. "Oral History: A Strategy that Works." *Social Education* 41 (May 1977): 378–381.

———. "Oral History Tells Its Own Story: The Development of the Loblolly Project." *The Social Studies* 68 (1977): 231–235.

Morrissey, Charles T. "Oral History: More than Tapes Are Spinning." *Library Journal* 105 (April 15, 1980): 932–933.

Reynolds, Sherrod. "Golden Hindesight, Homespun, Lagniappe, et al." *Teacher* 96 (March 1979): 68–71.

Rosenthal, Bob. "The Interview and Beyond: Some Methodological Questions for Oral Historians." *The Public Historian* 1 (Spring 1979): 58–67.

Ryant, Carl. "Oral History and Family History." *Family Heritage* (April 1979): 50–53.

Schockley, Allen. "Oral History: A Research Tool for Black History." *Negro History Bulletin* 41 (January/February 1978): 787–789.

Sitton, Thad. "Black History from the Community: The Strategies of Fieldwork." *The Journal of Negro Education* 50, no. 2 (Spring 1981): 171–181.

———. "Bridging the School-Community Gap: The Lessons of Foxfire." *Educational Leadership* 38, no. 3 (1980): 248–250.

———. "The Descendants of Foxfire." *The Oral History Review* (1978): 20–35.

———. "The Fire that Lit Up Learning." *Teacher* (March 1979): 65–67.

———. "Public Schools and Public History." *The Educational Forum* 54, no. 3 (March 1980): 277–283.

Susskind, J. "Oral History: A New Name for an Old Way of Learning." *Clearinghouse* 52 (December 1978): 179–180.

Winther, Ingred. "Family and Community History through Oral History." *The Public Historian* 1 (Summer 1979): 29–39.

Books That Use Oral History

Banks, Ann. *First Person America*. New York: Alfred A. Knopf, 1980.

Baskin, John. *New Burlington: The Life and Death of an American Village*. New York: W. W. Norton, 1976.

Brooks, Courtney G.; Grimwood, James M.; and Swenson, Loyd S., Sr. *Chariots for Apollo: A History of Manned Lunar Spacecraft*. Washington, D.C.: NASA, 1979.

Cooper, Patricia, and Buferd, Norma Bradley. *The Quilters: Women and Domestic Art, An Oral History*. Garden City, N.Y.: Doubleday, 1978.

Coyle, Laurie; Hershatter, Gail; and Honig, Emily. *Women at Farah: An Unfinished Story*. El Paso, Tex.: Reforma, 1979.

Cusick, Phillip A. *Inside High School: The Student's World*. Nashville, Tenn.: American Association for State and Local History, 1974.

Erikson, Kai T. *Everything in Its Path: Destruction of Community in the Buffalo Creek Flood*. New York: Touchstone, 1978.

Evans, George Ewart. *The Days that We Have Seen*. London: Faber and Faber, Ltd., 1975.

Gallagher, Dorothy. *Hannah's Daughters: Six Generations of an American Family, 1876–1976*. New York: Thomas Crowell, 1976.

Gluck, Sherna. *From Parlor to Prison: Five American Suffragists Talk about Their Lives*. New York: Vintage Press, 1976.

Gwaltney, John Langston. *Drylongso: A Self-Portrait of Black America*. New York: Random House, 1980.

Haley, Alex. *Roots*. New York: Doubleday, 1976.

Hareven, Tamara K. *Amoskeag: Life and Work in an American Factory-City*. New York: Pantheon Books, 1978.

Hoopes, Roy. *Americans Remember the World War II Home Front*. New York: Hawthorn Books, 1977.

Jellison, Charles A. *Tomatoes Were Cheaper: Tales from the Thirties*. Syracuse, N.Y.: Syracuse University Press, 1977.

Joseph, Peter. *Good Times: An Oral History of America in the Nineteen Sixties*. New York: William Morrow, 1974.

Kahn, Kathy. *Hillbilly Women*. New York: Doubleday, 1972.

Kearns, Doris. *Lyndon Johnson and the American Dream*. New York: Harper and Row, 1976.

Ladurie, Emmanuel Le Roy. *Montaillou: The Promised Land of Error*, trans. Barbara Bray. New York: Random House, 1979.

Lash, Joseph P. *Eleanor and Franklin*. New York: W. W. Norton, 1971.

Lewis, Oscar. *The Children of Sanchez: Autobiography of a Mexican Family*. New York: Random House, 1961.

Massey, Ellen Gray, ed. *Bittersweet Country*. Garden City, N.Y.: Doubleday, 1978.

McComb, David G. *Big Thompson: Profile of a Natural Disaster*. Boulder, Colo.: Pruett Publishing Co., 1980.

Miller, Merle. *Lyndon: An Oral Biography*. New York: Putnam's, 1980.

Montell, William L. *The Saga of Coe Ridge: A Study in Oral History*. Knoxville: University of Tennessee Press, 1970.

Namias, June. *First Generation: Oral Histories of Twentieth-Century American Immigrants*. Boston, Mass.: Beacon Press, 1978.

Robinson, John L. *Living Hard: Southern Americans in the Great Depression*. Washington, D.C.: University Press of America, 1981.

Rosengarten, Theodore. *All God's Dangers: The Life of Nate Shaw*. New York: Alfred A. Knopf, 1974.

Russo, David J. *Families and Communities: A New View of American History*. Nashville, Tenn.: American Association for State and Local History, 1974.

Schlesinger, Arthur M., Jr. *Robert Kennedy and His Times*. Boston, Mass.: Houghton Mifflin, 1978.

Terkel, Studs. *Division Street: America*. New York: Pantheon, 1966.

————. *Hard Times: An Oral History of the Great Depression*. New York: Pantheon, 1970.

————. *Working: People Talk about What They Do All Day and How They Feel about What They Do*. New York: Pantheon, 1974.

Terrill, Tom E., and Hirsch, Jerrold, eds. *Such as Us: Southern Voices of the Thirties*. Chapel Hill: University of North Carolina Press, 1978.

Wigginton, Eliot, ed. *I Wish I Could Give My Son a Wild Raccoon*. Garden City, N.Y.: Doubleday, 1976.

————, ed. *The Foxfire Book*. Garden City, N.Y.: Doubleday, 1972 (subsequent volumes by the same title).

Williams, T. Harry. *Huey P. Long*. New York: Alfred A. Knopf, 1969.

Wood, Pamela, ed. *The Salt Book*. Garden City, N.Y.: Doubleday, 1977.